PRAYING

ROBERT FARICY

SCM PRESS LTD

334 01281 3

First published 1979 by Villa Books
Reissued 1983 by SCM Press Ltd
26–30 Tottenham Road, London N1

Photoset in the United States
and printed in Great Britain by
Richard Clay (The Chaucer Press) Ltd
Bungay, Suffolk

Contents

"ABIDE IN ME"

Christian praying is in and through Jesus; he is our way to the Father. In Jesus, God reaches out to us, calling us to respond. That response is: to *be* in Jesus, to *abide* in Jesus.

In John's Gospel, Jesus just before his death tells his disciples that he is the true vine (Jn 15:1-9). The vine exists in the branches, and the branches have their existence as part of the vine. The vine-branches image describes the mutual presence-in-one-another of Jesus and us; he is in us and we are in him.

John 15:1-9 contains two directives. The first is to remain in Jesus, to abide in his love. The second follows from remaining in him; we should ask for whatever we want. The other points in the passage, like the efficacy of asking for what we want, depend on remaining in Jesus: bearing fruit, being pruned, becoming his disciples.

Jesus calls me, then, to abide in him. He calls me to an intimate personal relationship with him. This relationship is a matter of *experience.* By experience I do not mean a passing emotional impact, but a personal involvement. The Lord calls me to experience him, to have an experiential relationship with him – not only to know about him, but to know *him,* as a person. The central expression of this relationship, and the activity in which it is chiefly experienced, is prayer.

Prayer is quite simple. Essentially, praying is

7

remaining in the Lord "unprotected", with no defenses.

Reading about prayer or writing about it, talking about prayer, thinking and wishing about prayer — these can screen me from the Lord, hide me from him. Praying is dropping all the screens to stand naked before God, to remain simply in the Lord. Prayer calls for my total presence to the Lord that he may take possession of me. And he will; this is prayer's point, and the reason I exist. But I have to want it, and with an overmastering desire.

> When you set yourself down to pray, WHAT DO YOU WANT? If you want God to take possession of you, then you are praying. That is all prayer is . . . I long to tell myself that the reason why I "can't pray" is that I've never been taught, the right books have passed me by, the holy guru never came down my street. Hence the eager interest in books and articles on prayer — all obscuring me from my lack of true desire . . . If you desire to stand surrendered before God, then you are standing there; it needs absolutely nothing else.[1]

This is not always easy. But it *is* simple: to abide in the Lord, poor and with no defenses, willing to be trimmed clean to bear more fruit.

This book aims at helping to pray. It depends on how it is used. It could, unfortunately, serve as a substitute for remaining in the Lord in real prayer. It could help rationalize the avoidance of directly facing him without defenses — ("after all, I am reading about prayer."). A book can describe prayer, represent prayer in a reasonable facsimile; and so it can be used as a substitute for prayer, the way someone might eat a wax apple instead of a real one. But that is not what it is for. The following chapters are meant to be helpful, to deepen awareness of the realities and the possibilities of prayer, to suggest ways of approaching prayer, and to encourage prayerful abiding in the Lord to be trimmed clean and to receive new life.

*   *   *

I welcome gladly this second printing of *Praying*. Many people have let me know how much the book has helped them, and many others have asked where to get it. Now, finally, thanks to SCM Press, it is available again. My gratitude, for this and for many other things, to John Bowden, Margaret Lydamore, Mark Hammer, Ros Bacon, and everyone else at SCM Press.

Robert Faricy, S.J.

The Pontifical Gregorian University
Rome

The Feast of Christ the King
November 21, 1982

Notes

[1] Wendy Mary Beckett, "Simple Prayer", *The Clergy Review,* 63 (1978), 43-44.

I. PRAYING IN THE SPIRIT

"When the Paraclete comes, the Spirit of truth who comes from the Father and whom I shall send to you from the Father, he will bear witness to me" (Jn 15:26).

Chapter One

PRAYER AND THE HOLY SPIRIT

Christian prayer is trinitarian. Because God exists in three persons, each equally divine and united in their being-God, christian prayer goes to one of the three persons, or to all three. Because prayer consists of entering consciously into personal relationship with God, and because God exists as three persons, christian prayer addresses the Trinity, the Father or Jesus or the Holy Spirit or all three.

Habitually, some of us think first of God as one, and then of that divine unity as being shared by Father, Son, and Spirit; we understand the Trinity as within the divine nature and within the oneness. The image is of a circle representing the one divine nature, one God, and containing a triangle standing for the Trinity, with each side representing one divine person. There is only one God, but each person in God is God; this is the mystery of the Trinity: that in one God there participate three persons, each fully God.

However, the earlier and certainly more biblical conception sees first the Father, Jesus, and the Spirit. The three persons form a divine community. Because each is God, their unity is perfect, a perfect oneness of God, one God. We can represent this understanding by a circle enclosed in a triangle; the oneness of God is seen as a result of the union of three persons, each fully God: In this conception, God is understood primarily as Trinity, as three divine persons, each completely distinct but not at all separate, united in a community of divine love. This view of God makes it easier to pray in an interpersonal way, in a relational way.

The Trinity is a community of love. The Father loves Jesus, and Jesus loves the Father. This mutual love between Jesus and the Father exists as a divine person, the Holy Spirit. The Holy Spirit proceeds from the Father and from Jesus as the love between them, and so Thomas Aquinas writes that a name for the Spirit is Love. Further, "The Father and the Son love us in the Holy Spirit."[1] The Spirit is Love, and a gift of love, sent in love by Jesus and the Father.

As the love between the Father and Jesus, the Spirit who is sent to us unites each of us to the Father and to Jesus. God dwelling in us, the Holy Spirit acts to join each of us always more closely to Jesus and to God the Father in a union of love. When the Holy Spirit lives in me, I am caught up into the love between Jesus and the Father, loving the Father in Jesus' love for the Father, the Spirit; and loving Jesus with the love that proceeds from the Father and from him to me, the Spirit of love. The Spirit makes me a member of the divine community, joins me to the communion of the Trinity so that I become, in Jesus, an adopted child of God the Father, a brother or sister of Jesus, and a member of that unity in Jesus which takes the form of "the people of God", his Body, "the temple of the Holy Spirit", "the vine and the branches".

In his commentary on the vine-branches teaching

14

in John's gospel, Cyril of Alexandria points out that we share in God's own divine nature when we remain in Jesus and in his love like branches on a vine, because

> . . . in fact, the Holy Spirit of Christ unites us to him (see I Jn 4:13) . . . As the stalk communicates to the branches the quality and the condition of its own nature, so the only begotten Word of God gives to people, and above all to those who are united with him in faith, his Spirit. He bestows on them all kinds of holiness, makes them relatives and sharers in his and the Father's nature, nourishes them with love, and pours into them the knowledge of all virtue and goodness.[2]

So that I can pray, Jesus and the Father send me their Holy Spirit and, through the Spirit, come to me and dwell in me (Jn 14:23). This divine indwelling changes me; I exist in a new way, in the Spirit, enabled by the Spirit in me to know and love God in a personal way. We call this new way of existing "grace".

Prayer is, first of all, God's grace, his gift. My prayer, even though my own activity, is a gift from God by which I enter into interpersonal relationship with him, a properly personal relationship in which I know and love God and in which I accept God's knowledge and love of me.

The Holy Spirit in the New Testament
Especially in Luke's gospel and in the Acts of the Apostles, the Holy Spirit acts as the power of God.

15

The angel tells Mary, "The Holy Spirit will come upon you, and the power of the Most High will overshadow you" (Lk 1:35). The Hebrew parallelism between "Holy Spirit" and "power of the Most High" indicates identity: the Holy Spirit *is* the power of God. Conceived through the overshadowing of the Spirit, Jesus begins his messianic mission in the Spirit (Lk 1:35-38). From the wilderness, Jesus returns to Galilee "in the power of the Spirit" (Lk 4:14) to read in the synagogue, "The Spirit of the Lord is upon me . . ." (Lk 4:18). "Anointed with the Holy Spirit and with power", he goes about "doing good and healing . . ." (Acts 10:38).

The power of the Spirit fills Elizabeth, Zechariah, and Simeon (Lk 1:41 and 67; 2:25-27), and each speaks out inspired by the Spirit. Jesus tells his apostles to "stay in the city until you are clothed with power from on high" (Lk 24:49); "you shall receive power when the Holy Spirit has come upon you" (Acts 1:8). Luke's gospel and the Acts of the Apostles insistently underline the Spirit as power and as giving power, especially the power to pray and to speak "the word of God with boldness" (Acts 4:31).

In Paul's Letter to the Ephesians, we are, in Christ, "sealed with the promised Holy Spirit" (Eph 1:13). In the Spirit, we have access through Christ to the Father (Eph 2:18). And, because we have the same Spirit (Eph 4:3-4; see I Cor 12:4), we grow together into "a dwelling place of God in the Spirit" (Eph 2:22), into the new temple where God lives and receives worship. In this temple, which we constitute in the Spirit, Paul urges us to "pray in the Spirit on every possible occasion", "all the time, asking for what is needed" (Eph 6:18), and to receive God's word from the Holy Spirit (Eph 6:17).

In the eighth chapter of his Letter to the Romans, Paul stresses even more the Spirit's role in our prayer as well as his role in the whole Christian life. Paul calls us to walk in the Spirit, to live according to the Spirit, and to set our minds on the things of the Spirit (Rom 8:4-6). "The Spirit of Life" sets us free from sin and death (Rom 8:1-2). He gives us life because he is the Spirit of the Father who has raised Jesus from the dead; he makes us belong to Christ, giving new life to our spirits, because he is the Spirit of Christ (Rom 8:9-11). Jesus and the Father have the same Spirit, are one in one Spirit,[3] and their Spirit guides us, moves us (Rom 8:14), and helps us in our prayer. "When we cannot find the words to pray well, the Spirit himself expresses our prayers in a way beyond words . . . and the prayers expressed by the Spirit accord with the mind of God" (Rom 8:26-27). He cries out in us and with us, "Abba, Father", showing us that we truly are God's children and heirs (Rom 8:15-17; Gal 4:5-7). He intercedes for us (Rom 8:27). In him we already possess the beginnings of the life that comes after this life, and he moves us ahead, helping us to grow, keeping us going and giving us hope as we groan prayerfully toward the time of our complete freedom in glory (Rom 8:23-25).

In John's Gospel, Jesus speaks of himself and the Father as "we": "The Father and I are one" (Jn 10:30); *"We* are one" (Jn 17:22). This "Divine We" extends to us: "Father, may they all be one in us, as you are in me and I am in you" (Jn 17:21). "If someone loves me, he will keep my word and my Father will love him; we shall come to him and make our home with him" (Jn 14:23). Sharing in the "Divine We" of Jesus and the Father through their Spirit in us, we become more *"we"*, more one, more united. The "Divine We" as such is the Holy Spirit, who relates the Father and Jesus, and us to them and to one another.[4]

John's Gospel, in Jesus' last supper farewell address, gives us an understanding of the Holy Spirit as Paraclete. John shows the Paraclete as the Holy Spirit in a special role, as the personal presence of Jesus in the Christian while Jesus is with the Father.[5] Jesus speaks of sending "another Paraclete" because he is the first Paraclete. The Spirit, then, is another Jesus. John's gospel wants to show not the difference between Jesus and the Holy Spirit, but the similarities. Jesus must depart before the Paraclete comes; the Paraclete makes Jesus present after he has gone to the Father. Just as Jesus and the Father are one (Jn 10:30), so too Jesus and the Spirit are one, and where the Paraclete is, there too are Jesus and the Father (Jn 14:23). Because we have in us the Paraclete, we have too the intimate presence of Jesus and of the Father, for Jesus and the Father are one.

What does the Holy Spirit as Paraclete do? "Paraclete" can be translated as "Counselor". The Paraclete teaches us: "The Paraclete, the Holy Spirit whom the Father will send in my name, will teach you everything and remind you of all I have said to you" (Jn 14:26). And he guides us: "Being the Spirit of truth, he will guide you along the way of all truth" (Jn 16:13). The Paraclete teaches and guides, brings truth to our understanding and to our judgement.

The Spirit who dwells in us is unknown to "the world", which cannot receive him, and neither sees nor knows him (Jn 14:17). The world stands against the Paraclete, not indifferent but hostile, because it stands convicted by him of its sin in not accepting Jesus, and it stands confronted by the Spirit with the righteousness of Jesus whom the world condemned to death. The ruler of this world, the "evil one" and in him all forces of evil, are judged defeated and powerless by the Paraclete (Jn 16:8-11). The Spirit, then, enlightens us as to the sinfulness of "the world" — of the world that rejects Christ, as to the righteousness of Jesus in whom we receive the Spirit of justice and holiness, and as to Jesus' victory over everything that oppresses us.

Besides teaching and guiding, and besides bringing to the light the truth about sin and righteousness and Jesus' victory, the Paraclete bears witness to Jesus (Jn 15:26). This teaching of Jesus comes just after a teaching about the hatred on the part of the world towards Jesus and the Father, and just before a teaching on the world's persecution of Jesus' disciples. The context makes clear that the Paraclete's witness-bearing infuriates all who reject Jesus and the Father. And the Paraclete's witness to Jesus comes through the witness of Jesus' followers: "and you are also witnesses" (Jn 15:27); this is why they will be put out of synagogues and even killed (Jn 16:2).

The Holy Spirit in Prayer

Jesus' Spirit in me, in my prayer, says "Yes" in me through Jesus to the Father. Jesus' Spirit guides my prayer, teaching me in hidden ways and delicately how to pray, how to remain in Jesus prayerfully. The Holy Spirit gives my prayer life power, efficacy, the life and power and efficacy not only of love but

19

of Love. The Spirit prays in me, for me, through me, and with me.

And the Holy Spirit brings sin and guilt to light, my own sin first of all. In prayer, to the extent that I pray without pretenses, unprotected by my usual facade, remaining in the Lord in all my weakness and sinfulness, the Lord with his Spirit of love burns away my filth, casts out the resistance in me to his love, and takes my fear, guilt, anger, and anxiety, filling with his Spirit of healing and consolation the places where they festered. As Jesus takes possession of me for himself and the Father in my prayer, as he fills me more with his Spirit, I will find myself called to give up some things, to change, and − in one way or another − to bear witness to Jesus.

Prayer can be dangerous; when it is real, prayer pits against me all in the world that rejects Jesus. Inevitably, if I truly pray, I will find myself called to bear witness to the Lord, to stand up and be counted. And so I will at some point find the cross of rejection, of misunderstanding, of the pain that the world, in rejecting Christ and those who in his Spirit bear him witness, can cause. In the strength of the Spirit, I can follow Jesus, taking up my cross.

The Holy Spirit makes my prayer a prayer of love; he joins the Father and Jesus, and he catches me up in their mutual love that he is. Through the Spirit Jesus dwells in me and I in him; Augustine writes: "We remain in Christ when we are his members, he remains in us when we are his temple."[6] John Henry Newman puts it in these words: "Christ Jesus . . . came once, then he ascended, he has come again. He came first in the flesh; he has come the second time in the Spirit."[7] Connected in the Spirit of love to Jesus, remaining in him, I can consciously relate to him, accept his loving presence and remain consciously and lovingly present in him. And this is prayer.

Jesus and the Father are one. Remaining in Jesus through his Spirit, I remain united with the Father, and I can go prayerfully to him as his child because I have the Spirit of his Son.

The Spirit, in my prayer, leads me to know Jesus and the Father personally, as persons. This knowledge takes place through love; it is a knowledge-through-love. The Holy Spirit leads me to a loving knowing, to a knowing through loving and being loved. This "knowing through love" can take the form of a dark knowledge, a knowing in obscurity that seems a non-knowing, a blank. It will often be a groping in the dark, a knowledge in the darkness of faith. Not a knowledge of facts nor a gaining of information, it depends not on ideas nor concepts but on the union of my will with the Father's, on the union of my heart with Jesus' heart, on union in the Holy Spirit.

And yet, the knowledge of God that comes in prayer is a real knowing, not less than knowing facts, but more. To know a person differs from knowing about that person. Of course, I want to know all I can about whom I love and who loves me; but, mainly, I want *more* than to know about them. I want to know *them*. Jesus and the Father know me personally by name, and perfectly, through and through; they love me, accepting me, utterly and unconditionally. Their Spirit leads me through love — through my acceptance of their love and through my loving response — to know them more deeply and to love them more.

This knowledge through love is not an abstract

idea; it is often obscure, but it is concrete. It is experiential. Prayer means experience of God, not just nor primarily intellectual experience, but affective experience in which the emotions play an important role. Feelings count. Certainly, I can and sometimes must pray without any particular feelings — there will be times when my prayer is quite dry — but feelings do matter. Ordinarily, my knowing the divine persons in prayer will be accompanied by love and by the spiritual taste that goes with love. It will be affective knowledge, a knowing that leads to loving and that takes place through loving and being loved.[8]

We can express what happens in prayer more accurately if we take into consideration that the action of the Spirit in prayer has by far the most important place. In prayer, no matter how I might feel about it, I find myself caught up in an event, a happening, that overspills my subjective consciousness. I do not really control that event, I am part of what happens. In prayer I enter more consciously into my relationship with God, into the community of the divine persons already living in me. I give myself over to action of the Spirit of Jesus. My prayer consists not principally of what I do, but rather of what the Holy Spirit does in me and with me and of my co-operation with his action. In practice, this means being small, childlike, peaceful and quiet, flexible, open to what Jesus wants, to whatever the Father calls me to, to how the Spirit leads me.

Prayer can be compared to a game in which more than one player participates. In a game, a certain discipline and observance of basic ground-rules form the presupposition of playing. What I do depends to a great extent on what the other players do. So in prayer; it is, like a game, an interpersonal happening. If I pray to Jesus, I engage myself in an active relationship with him, analogous to playing a game with him. I need, then, to take him seriously as part of the overall activity, and to be open and ready to move with his Spirit. Just as when the players play, the game happens, so when I remain consciously in Jesus, open to his action in me and to the leading of his Spirit, prayer happens.

Prayer might also be compared to dying. Like Christian death, prayer is a surrender of my own spirit to God, a going out of myself to God already present in me and to me. On the cross, Jesus, in an act of love and abandonment to the Father, prays, "Father, into your hands I commend my spirit." (Lk 23:46). And Stephen, in the moment of his martyrdom, prays, "Lord Jesus, receive my spirit" (Acts 7:56). When I pray, I give over my own spirit, in the Spirit of Jesus and the Father, letting the Spirit in me and with me, say "Yes".

The Spirit and Holiness

The Holy Spirit is a gift of sanctification.[9] He leads us to holiness. What is holiness? Holiness is the infinite capacity to love and to receive love. Only God is truly holy, because only God is infinite. But I am called to grow in holiness, to grow in the capacity to love God and to receive God's love, to grow in the capacity to love others and to receive their love. My growth in the capacity to love and to receive love is what the Holy Spirit does in me; he sanctifies me, helps me to grow in holiness, in love.

Notes

[1] Thomas Aquinas, I *Sent.*, d. 32, q. 1, a. 3; see *Summa theologiae*, I, q. 43, a. 2c and *ad* 3, a. 3 *ad* 3; also *Summa theologiae*, I, q. 37, a. 1 *ad* 2, *ad* 3; I *Sent.*, d. 31, q. a. 1; *Contra Gentiles*, IV, c. 21.

[2] Migne, Greek Series, vol. 74, 331-334.

[3] Phil 1:19; Rom 8:9; Gal 4:6; II Cor 3:17b; II Thess 2:8; all these speak, somehow, of the Spirit as of Jesus. The Spirit is "the Spirit of God" in I Cor 2:11 and Rom 8:11 and 14.

[4] Heribert Muhler, "The Person of the Holy Spirit", in *The Holy Spirit and Power*, ed. K. McDonnell (New York: Doubleday, 1975), p. 27.

[5] Raymond E. Brown, *The Gospel according to John, The Anchor Bible* (New York: Doubleday, 1970), p. 1139.

[6] *In Joannis Evangelium tractatus centum viginti quatuor*, Migne, Latin Series, vol. 35, 1379.

[7] *Lectures on the Doctrine of Justification* (London: Longmans, 1874; first published 1838), p. 205.

[8] Some of the material so far in this chapter is partly based on scholarly historical studies, particularly of medieval texts; especially: O. Brooke, "The Trinitarian Aspect of the Ascent of the Soul to God in the Theology of William of St. Thierry", *Recherches de théologie ancienne et médiévale*, 26 (1959), 87-127; R. Faricy, "The Trinitarian Indwelling", *The Thomist*, 35 (1971), 369-404; J. Dedek, *"Quasi experimentalis cognitio:* A Historical Approach to the Meaning of St. Thomas", *Theological Studies*, 22 (1961), 357-390.

[9] Thomas Aquinas, *Summa theologiae*, I, q. 43, a. 7.

Chapter Two

PRAYER OF DISCERNMENT

The Lord sends us his Holy Spirit of truth to guide us into the truth (Jn 16:13). Christianity is not just a set of truths but a way of life; and living involves choices. The Holy Spirit guides us not just to true facts and true beliefs, but to the truth-to-be-done, to correct decisions. He teaches us not only what is true but how to choose truly, how to make the right decisions, and so how to act in truth. The process of arriving through prayer and under the guidance of the Spirit at a right decision regarding a specific course of action is called "spiritual discernment" or, more frequently, "discernment".[1]

What Is Discernment?
The practice of discernment goes back to Christianity's earliest beginnings, to Jesus' promise to send us a Counselor, to Paul's encouragement to let the Spirit lead us (Rom 8:14), to John's advice to "test the spirits to see whether they are of God" (I Jn 4:1). In christian tradition, discernment means choosing the way of the light of Jesus Christ rather than the way of darkness, and choosing prayerfully the concrete here and now options that come from his Spirit and that lead to him. Sometimes writers refer to "discernment of the Spirit", because discernment regards understanding how the Holy Spirit leads us. God speaks to us in many ways: through the Bible, through our friends, in our work, in all the events of

25

everyday living; and he speaks to us through his guiding Spirit. Discernment involves prayerfully bringing to the light the decisions that our life calls on us to make and seeing which way the Spirit leads us to decide. Which one of two or more options comes from the Lord? Which decisions does God in his holy will want us to make regarding life's circumstances now?

But various "spirits" can influence us. We have to "test the spirits" to see which come from God. And so, often, Christian tradition speaks of "the discernment of spirits", discernment to determine which is the voice of the Holy Spirit, to understand which impulses and "leadings" come from him and which do not, so that we can come to the choices that the Lord chooses for us.

Discernment differs from prudence. Both concern making decisions, but prudence judges the act itself, whether a given action or option is wise, prudent under the circumstances. Discernment judges the *impulse* to act, judges whether the idea to do this comes from God or from elsewhere. There should arise no conflict, of course, between the demands of true prudence and the conclusions of discernment. However, what the Lord calls us to do will not always square with "prudence" understood in a worldly sense, as necessary conformity with conventional ways of acting.

Ordinarily discernment will regard personal decisions, will concern the question, "What does the Lord want *me* to decide or to do in this particular case?" Sometimes, according to our responsibilities, we may have to help others to discern God's will; pastoral counselors, spiritual directors, parents, psychologists, may be called to do this. I may be called to pray with a friend, with my wife or my husband, or with my brother or sister, to discern what the Spirit says to him or to her. Parents may have to discern for their children. And all of us have to make our own decisions; the Lord has given us his Spirit to guide us.

Norms for Discerning

How can we judge what comes from God and what comes from "the world, the flesh, or the devil" — from a spirit of worldliness that opposes God, or from disordered or sinful inclinations in ourselves, or from the devil and his minions? What criteria do we have? We have objective norms, norms that go beyond us and exist outside us; and we have subjective norms, our own interior feelings, thoughts, and impulses. Both are important.

Objectively, God gives us his Word in the Bible and in the doctrines and teachings of the Church. If the conclusion of a discernment goes against these, one must obviously question and re-examine the discernment process. God does not contradict himself. In a more general way, the decisions of legitimate authority provide an objective norm for discernment. Usually, however, the objective norms do not guide us sufficiently in judging proposals for possible concrete action. Clearly, Church teaching can show me the error of an impulse to steal or to commit adultery, if my union with the Lord is so weak as to permit any consideration of such an action. Circumstances may simply remove me from this situation, or my superiors acting within their responsibilities may give me a new assignment with no room for discussion, and I can see the hand of God in this. But I will often have to rely on "subjective" criteria for deciding between two or more possible avenues of action both of which seem good. The Spirit of Jesus can guide me, through my prayer, to choose the best — that which conforms to God's loving will for me in this particular case.

The interior or "subjective" norms for discerning are not subjective in the sense of being arbitrary; they are rooted in the action of the Spirit in the interior of the "subject", of the person prayerfully seeking the will of God in a particular matter. According to Ignatius of Loyola, who formulated rules for discerning and for arriving at decisions and who has had a great influence on contemporary writers, the chief norm for judging whether a particular interior impulse or idea or movement is from the Holy Spirit is what he calls "consolation". By consolation he means *facility in relating to God,* a certain relative ease in finding the Lord in prayer precisely in terms of this particular interior movement or idea. This facility or ease in finding the Lord can take the form of joy, or of a relatively greater sentiment of love for the Lord. It can be a feeling of peace and "rightness" about this particular decision. It might take the form of tears, or of sorrow for sin and of repentance. It might be just a subtle feeling that the Lord wants this from me now.

Discernment in Practice
If I want to discern God's will in an important matter, I must take the preliminary step of gathering the facts, the pertinent information. I may need to look at books or to consult with someone. I must marshal the pros and the cons so that I have an adequate grasp of the problem.

And then I bring the matter to the Lord in an explicit way. I have already prayed for light and guidance when informing myself of the facts. But now I present my possible decisions to the Lord. He is Lord, and I want to bring my decision-making consciously into the zone of his lordship, under his lordship. I try to think the decision through with the Lord, not so much using a carefully ordered and logical rational approach — I have done that in the preliminary fact-gathering phase — but mulling over my alternative decisions, pondering my various options and their possible consequences. I do this while, as it were, looking the Lord in the eye. I raise up to him, in turn, the different possibilities. And I see how I feel about each in terms of my relationship with the Lord.

Ordinarily, over a period of time that might depend on the importance of the decisions in question, I will feel a certain fittingness or rightness regarding one particular course of action when I "look the Lord in the eye" and lift up that possible decision to him. I may feel a relative peace with him in terms of deciding in that particular way. My peace may overflow in joy, gladness, delight. At any rate, I hope to find one of the alternative decisions in terms of which I find comparative facility in relating prayerfully to the Lord, one answer that I feel especially comfortable with when I present that answer to the Lord in prayer.

I can depend on the Holy Spirit present within me. He will guide me into a knowledge-through-love, into a felt knowledge, to a judgement that I feel in my heart. Usually the inspirations of the Holy Spirit resemble the natural impulses of my mind and my will. What distinguishes the thoughts and feelings

29

that are rooted in the Spirit is the love that infuses them, the love poured into my heart by the Holy Spirit. The problem is this: I can easily mistake my own natural likes, dislikes, affections, feelings and thoughts for the inspirations of the Spirit. This is why I need time to sift things through with the Lord in prayer, because the touches of his Spirit are often subtle and not easy to discern.

Yet, the peace, love and joy that come from God are quite unlike any that come from human sources alone. Edward O'Connor writes that as a person grows in the Spirit

> . . . and becomes more and more accustomed to these fruits of the Spirit, he becomes more sure in recognizing them and in discerning the action of the divine Spirit by means of them. But until a person has developed a kind of sense for the action of God, it is difficult for him to make use of these signs with any sureness. There is a complacency that may pass for peace, and there are false joys and wrong kinds of love that may be mistaken for those of the Spirit.[2]

I cannot be absolutely sure of the conclusion of my discernment. I try to understand what decision the Lord wants me to take, and then I take that decision knowing that I am in his hands and that if I make a mistake in judgement I can trust him to take care of me. But after I have arrived at a conclusion, at a decision, I hold that decision up to the Lord, asking him to verify it for me. And I judge the decision verified to the extent that I find facility in relating to the Lord in terms of my decision, to the extent that he gives me peace, or joy, or an increase in love, or a certain sureness that this is truly what he wants.

Some decisions call for communal discernment.[3] Husband and wife, or a whole family, after discussing a possible decision, can pray together seeking the Lord's will — each praying privately at the same time, or all praying together, or both successively, and then, if there is consensus, holding up their decision to the Lord together for verification. If after sufficient prayer no consensus is reached, a decision may still have to be made; but at least the Lord has been consulted, the decision has been prayed over. Any small group or community can do the same thing; larger groups, such as chapters of religious congregations, might need a somewhat more step-by-step approach in arriving at a decision.

As I grow in union with God, I will find that the inspirations of the Holy Spirit will tend to be more an atmosphere that envelops my whole life. Ordinarily I will, without taking any special steps, plan and judge according to the Spirit. I will learn more and more "to walk in the Spirit" (Rom 8:4), to live and to make all my decisions under his influence. Yet, there will be times when I wonder what the Lord is asking of me, and when I will need to turn to him, bringing matters more explicitly under his lordship and listening with special care to his Spirit.

"Good" and "Bad" Spirits
In his "Rules for the Discernment of Spirits",[4] Ignatius Loyola speaks of "the good spirit" and "the bad spirit". What comes from "the good spirit" is whatever comes from God, from his Holy Spirit.

What comes from "the bad spirit" is whatever comes from the world, the flesh, or the devil. Not every inspiration comes from the Spirit of Jesus. An impulse or an idea can come from myself, from my own worldliness, from my conformity with the spirit of this world rather than with the Holy Spirit. Or it can come from my own disordered inclinations, from my timidity, my pride, my need for attention, or my love of money and possessions; or from my fear of failure, my anxiety, my ambition, or my anger or resentment.

And an impulse or idea can come from the devil and the evil spirits who follow him. The devil can imitate an angel of light and present himself in ways that appeal to our weaknesses, especially to the weaknesses we least like to admit. But, as St Ignatius points out, the devil is a coward, and runs when faced squarely. We can discover him, because what comes from the devil lacks love, it has a grating quality, and it leads to turmoil and confusion. We can take the authority that God gives us, rebuking the devil, ordering him to leave in Jesus' name. And we should do this, whether he tempts us in more or less obvious ways, or whether he comes with apparently good and virtuous thoughts and urges.

The Lord calls all of us to prayerfully seek his will in discernment. But to a few people he gives a special gift, a charism, to distinguish what comes from the Holy Spirit and what comes from other sources. These, then, possess the gift of discernment to an extraordinary degree. The First Letter to the Corinthians speaks of this charism when it describes "the varieties of gifts" that are distributed by God and that include "the ability to distinguish between spirits" (I Cor 12:10).

In today's world, and even sometimes in Christianity, one finds a dominant tendency to belittle the possibility of anything outside the world's experience having an influence on us. Evil spirits, however, do exist. Much more importantly, God acts in our lives. He reacts to our prayers. If I speak to him, he will somehow respond. And he sends his Spirit into my heart to counsel me, to guide me in my decisions. In a rationalistic world, the Lord wants me to search his loving will. In a materialistic world, he calls me to listen to his Spirit, who teaches me to discern and to interpret his action in my life now (Lk 12:56).[5]

Notes

[1] The literature on discernment remains somewhat sparse. The most useful treatments that I have found are: William S. Kurz, S.J., "Discernment as 'Walking in the Spirit' ", *The Bible Today*, 91 (1977), 1268-1272; and Edward O'Connor, C.S.C., "Discernment of Spirits", an article in three parts in three successive issues of *New Covenant*, vol. 4, no. 10 (April 1975), pp. 10-13; no. 11 (May 1975), pp. 31-33; and no. 12 (June 1975), pp. 26-29. A good study in the Ignatian tradition of discernment is that of John Carroll Futrell, S.J., "Ignatian Discernment", *Studies in the Spirituality of Jesuits*, 2 (1970), 47-88. See also the excellent article of John R. Sheets, S.J., "Profile of the Spirit: A Theology of Discernment of Spirits", *Review for Religious*, 30 (1971), 363-376; also, Thomas A. Dunne, S.J., "Models of Discernment", *The Way Supplement*, 23 (Autumn 1974), 18-27; and James Walsh, S.J., "Discernment of the Spirit", *U.I.S.G. Bulletin*, 22 (4th quarter, 1971), 13-18. For the historical background especially, see Jacques Guillet *et al.*, *Discernment of Spirits*, trans. Sister Innocentia Edwards, ed. Edward Malatesta, S.J. (Collegeville: Liturgical Press, 1970); this is a translation of the article "Discernment des éprits" in the *Dictionnaire de Spiritualite*, vol. 3 (Paris: Beauchesne, 1957), cols. 1222-1291.

[2] Edward O'Connor, C.S.C., "Discernment of Spirits", part 3, pp. 27-28.

33

[3] On communal discernment in groups of more than a few people, see: Jules J. Toner, S.J., "A Method of Communal Discernment of God's Will", *Studies in the Spirituality of Jesuits,* 3 (1971), 121-152; John Carroll Futrell, "Communal Discernment: Reflections on Experience", *Studies in the Spirituality of Jesuits,* 4 (1972), 159-192; John Carroll Futrell, "To Be Together ... in Spite of Everything", *Review for Religious,* 32 (1973), 514-521. On communal discernment in general, see Francis Martin, "Communal Discernment", *Community Spiritual Leadership: Donum Dei,* 18 (Ottawa: Canadian Religious Conference, 1971), 49-66; William C. Spohn, "Charismatic Communal Discernment and Ignatian Communities", *The Way Supplement,* 20 (Autumn 1973), 38-54; William C. Spohn, "Communal Discernment", *New Covenant,* vol. 4, no. 10 (April 1975), pp. 14-17.

[4] *Spiritual Exercises,* numbers 313-336.

[5] Discernment is an example of bringing everything in my life under the lordship of Jesus so that I grow in being centered on him and in integration of life; see R. Faricy, S.J., *Spirituality for Religious Life* (New York: Paulist, 1976), Chapter Two, "Faith and Integration", pp. 15-26.

Chapter Three
PRAYER AND GROWTH

Jesus introduces his teaching on prayer in Luke's Gospel by saying "When you pray . . .". He continues by teaching us the Lord's Prayer, encouraging us to ask for what we need, and concludes, "How much more will the heavenly Father give the Holy Spirit to those who ask him" (Lk 11: 13b). John's Gospel has the same teaching in a more developed way. In Jesus' last discourse, the two passages about Jesus as the true vine and the sending of the Spirit are bracketed by two almost identical encouragements: "Whatever you ask in my name, I will do it" (Jn 14:13-14) and "Whatever you ask the Father in my name, he will give it to you" (Jn 15:16b). Jesus tells us to ask for his Spirit so that we can remain in him and so that we can pray.

Growth in prayer, in conscious union with God, is grace, and like all grace it depends on the presence of the Spirit. A greater outpouring of the Holy Spirit, a fuller presence of the Spirit, results in progress in prayer because it causes closer union with God. We can and should ask for the Holy Spirit, and in greater abundance, so that we may grow in prayer. The Holy Spirit is the great Gift.

The danger in all other gifts lies in that I can use them selfishly, make minor idols of the gifts and, perhaps without adverting to the fact, become more attached to the Lord's gifts than to the Lord. This holds true especially for spiritual gifts, such as gifts of prayer; and all prayer is a gift, whether I recognize it as such or not. I cannot help my attachment to gifts of prayer, to praise, to joy, to consolation and peace, to awareness of the Lord's presence, to a kind of ease and facility in praying. I naturally tend to like these, to form attachments to them. The Lord calls me to himself more strongly than he calls me to gifts of prayer, to want him and the gift of his Holy Spirit more than the gifts that result from the Spirit's presence in me. He calls me to love with an open hand, not clinging to his gifts of prayer, not holding on tight to consolations or happy feelings, but clinging to him, holding on to him in his Spirit, letting him guide my prayer, happy to let him love me the way he wants to love me at the time. He calls me to freedom in his Spirit. How I feel will, naturally, matter to me, but I depend on God, not on my feelings; without such freedom, without total dependence on God in my prayer, growth in prayer bogs down in unfreedom and in gluttony for experiences.

The Spirit of prayer is the Spirit of freedom. Freedom comes from searching only for "the one thing necessary", "the better part" that Mary chooses in preference to busily doing many things. The one thing necessary consists in remaining in the Lord, sitting like Mary at his feet, looking at him, receiving his word, remaining in his love (Lk 11:39-42).

The Process of Growth

Prayer is remaining in the Lord, being united with him; in one sense prayer is an end in itself with no purpose beyond itself, because God created us to be united with him, and beyond that union lies no further goal. But in another sense, prayer's purpose remains always outside prayer itself, ahead of it, because prayer is a process leading toward an always fuller union with the Lord and a deeper remaining in him. Prayer, then, is a union that grows always closer and deeper.

In prayer, the initiative belongs to the Lord; he gives the beginnings and he gives the growth. Growth in prayer takes different forms for different persons, and for the same persons it takes different forms at different times. The general path of prayer's progress has been traced particularly by the Carmelite tradition stemming from Teresa of Avila and John of the Cross. The past few decades have seen greatly increased study of the teachings of the two Carmelite reformers, translations of their works, commentaries and adaptations.

What form, in general, does the trajectory of prayer take? What long-term path does progress in prayer ordinarily take? The descriptions one finds for instance in manuals of the spiritual life are not so helpful; they tend to name states rather than to describe what goes on. Names help little, but descriptions of experience together with practical advice can illuminate personal experience in prayer. John of the Cross and Teresa of Avila do this, and without too much concern for technical labels. They do, however, belong to another century, culture, language, mentality, and type of society; and they both wrote principally for Carmelite contemplatives with a quite different lifestyle from that of most people today.

I have found useful two contemporary descriptions of growth in prayer. Ruth Burrows, a Carmelite nun, has written a simple but profound, wise, and light-giving description of prayer's path: *Guidelines for Mystical Prayer.*[2] Quite practical, it stands as a modern handbook that can guide us no matter what our state in life or our background. Shorter, concise, and perhaps somewhat too simple, although helpful, is Yves Raguin's *Paths of Contemplation,* Chapters 5 to 21, which takes prayer from "the first steps" to the last stages.[3]

Both these books describe the trajectory of growth in prayer. Speaking generally, this path moves in the direction of an always greater simplicity. The emphasis changes gradually from thinking to loving, from the understanding to the will, from conceptualization to simply looking lovingly at the Lord. What I have just written over-simplifies the process of growth in prayer, but it gives the basic dynamic: from more activity on the part of the person praying to more receptivity; from interior acts and thoughts to a simpler stance of contemplation; from less experience of being actively and personally involved with the Lord to more; from dependence on one's own activities in prayer to more dependence on the action of the Holy Spirit.

For anyone who prays seriously, who for example faithfully gives a substantial amount of time every day to just be with the Lord, say even forty minutes or an hour, this is the Lord's plan, to draw that person into an always closer experience of himself. I mean experience in the sense of personal involvement with the Lord, in the sense that we speak of the need for a doctor to have medical experience or of an experienced spiritual director, in the sense that unless beliefs become real in terms of practical human experience they mean little for progress in union with God.

Peaks and Valleys

The same creative imagination that formed the story of the prodigal son, the sermon on the mount and the liturgy of the last supper works in the Lord's relationship with every person who reaches out to him in prayer. Relationship with the Lord in prayer follows the path that he plans, and the paths differ according to how the Lord acts with each person. The delicacy of God, his respect for the individual person and for the person's freedom and personal autonomy, his generous response to any acceptance of his invitation to believe or to be healed or to walk with him – these qualities of God with regard to us fill the pages of the gospels. And we find these same attributes in the Lord's action in our prayer. Prayer is a relationship, a dialogue, a two-way street; it has a dynamism and a movement that depends on the persons involved. It has its ups and its downs, its peaks and its valleys.

Strong experiences of conversion or of healing can take place, even in those who think themselves already sufficiently converted and adequately healed; these peak experiences mark a new beginning for prayer. The Lord, a Lord of surprises, can come in a manifest way with his overwhelming love and with his gifts when we do not expect him and, when we do expect him, in unanticipated ways. "Peaks" in relationship with the Lord take various forms. They can come during the time of a silent retreat, in a time of grief or after a serious set-back, in a moment or over a period of a few days in regular daily prayer. They heal us and convert us; we feel that, up to now, nothing has happened, and it all begins here. And, truly, such a peak in prayer does initiate something new.

A classic contemporary peak experience that begins a new prayerful relationship with the Lord, and a good example of a strong converting and healing touch of the Lord, takes place in the pentecostal tradition — in pentecostalism, in neo-pentecostalism, and in the charismatic renewal — in the form of the "baptism in the Spirit". Granted that everyone receives the Holy Spirit in the reception of the sacrament of baptism, and that the so-called "baptism in the Spirit" is not a true sacrament in the sense of baptism by water, the fact remains that something important happens. It "initiates a decisively new sense of the powerful presence and working of God in one's life",[4] and so appears as paradigmatic for peaks in prayer.

In the New Testament, "to baptize in the Spirit" means "to pour out the Spirit", "to give the Spirit", "to send the Spirit". The word "baptism", used metaphorically, does not necessarily refer to sacramental baptism but to a powerfully operative grace that changes a person's life by changing the relationship with God. So anyone can baptize sacramentally, but only God can "baptize in the Spirit", only God can give grace.

What happens to someone "baptized in the Spirit"? What results does such a grace have in that person's life? A friend wrote to me that he discovered "a new thirst for prayer, a new love for others, and an active concern for their discovering the Lord, a new recollection, faith, joy, peace; all this surprised me because I had put so much effort into it for years, and the results had been poor." A priest had this to say in a recent letter:

I had two serious spiritual problems. The first, that I did not seem to be able to give myself *totally* to the Lord. The second, more complex, consisted of doubts about the authenticity of my vocation. Briefly, I was a priest faithful to his duties, resigned to live the faith in a Godless world; I didn't even hope to be able to have a true and strong experience of God.

After being prayed with by some friends for a new outpouring of the Holy Spirit, he "experienced an unimagined freedom that came from deep inside me; in that freedom I finally gave myself entirely to the Lord, and my whole heart proclaimed that Jesus is Lord."

Another friend writes of such an outpouring of the Spirit during his annual retreat:

I praised the Lord and thanked him all day, and couldn't stop thanking him. The next day, as soon as I began to ask forgiveness for my sins, I felt the Lord free me right down to the roots. I felt freed from chains that tied and slowed me, from bonds I hadn't even known existed. When you pull on a spider web, you discover a whole network of threads that were hidden from sight, and you finally get rid of the insect itself that wove the web. A painless operation, and afterward I felt amazingly light, free. A prodigal child, loved by the Father who remade me, filled me, and cared for me lovingly and attentively.

The "peaks" in relationship with God, these new and powerful sendings of his Spirit in our hearts, come infrequently. Any quite strong and life-changing experience of the Lord, any such great grace, leaves us "new creatures". Lesser "peaks" can come more frequently, moments when the Lord touches us in a special way, or times – even days or months – when the Lord gives us quite special treatment. But we would not recognize the peaks if there were no valleys.

John of the Cross describes "nights" that come, in one way or another, into everyone's prayer life; these are the valleys, and like the peaks they come in a great variety of ways and shapes. Darkness in prayer, a sense of aloneness, a sense of God's absence or at least a lack of awareness of his loving presence, a feeling of walking in the desert far from the living waters – these experiences purify us; they form part of the Lord's pedagogy in teaching us to pray and in getting us closer to him. In their own way, then, they too are grace. A "night" in prayer can last a long time, months, or even several years. Many factors can be involved causally: physical or psychological illness, failure in some important area of life, external pressures. To the extent that we let him, the Lord purifies us through these darknesses and drynesses.

The Lord calls me to let him love me the way he wants to love me at the time. If in darkness, then I can sit quietly and as peacefully as I can in the darkness with him, feeling perhaps nothing but knowing in faith that even if I walk in a valley of darkness he is beside me, guiding me. Fretting, kicking against the goad, will prove counterproductive. If the darkness is caused by some sinful attachment on my part, I should break that attachment and try to reform my life. If I remain unaware of any particular sinful attachment, feeling only my own general sinfulness and spiritual inadequacy, then I can simply accept the dark as a purifying grace.

"My father is the gardener . . . any branch that bears fruit, he trims clean to make it bear more fruit" (Jn 15:2).

Obstacles to Growth

Why do many who do pray seriously seem to make little progress? Why, as John of the Cross points out, do so few enter real contemplation? To put it another way, why, when Jesus came, did so many religious people reject him while so many sinners and poor simple people opened their hearts to him? God wants to give himself to us entirely and without reserve, not just to some but to everyone; he created us for that. So the obstacles are not on his side, but on ours. What are they?

The biggest obstacle is self-complacency that blocks out full practical trust in the Lord and in his love. I do not mean having a good "self-image" but, rather, having a false image of oneself, having a prideful complacency that will not bend, will not become small and child-like and trusting. Paul uses a text from Isaiah to describe this being closed to the Lord; speaking to the Jewish leaders, he quotes the Old Testament:

You shall indeed hear but never
    understand,
and you shall indeed see but never
    perceive.
For this people's heart has grown numb,

> and their ears are heavy of hearing,
> and their eyes they have closed;
> lest they should perceive with their eyes,
> and hear with their ears,
> and understand with their heart,
> and be converted,
> and I will heal them.
>
> (Acts 28:27; see Is 6:10)

Jesus quotes the same text to the leaders of Israel: "He has blinded their eyes and dulled their heart, for fear that they see with their eyes and understand with their heart, and I will heal them" (Jn 12:40).

This spiritual blindness and deafness, this deadness of heart, blocks our progress in prayer. What is the solution? It lies at two levels: what we can do and what God does. What can we do? We can follow the christian teaching from the beginning that "our eye be single", that we want God more than anything else. Teresa of Avila writes that the most important thing is an absolute and unshakable determination not to stop before arriving at the source of living waters no matter what happens and no matter what it costs and no matter how others may criticize: to get there or to die trying.[5] This firm determination can become rigid or fanatical unless it grounds itself in humility and simplicity.

At the level of what the Lord does, we have his promise, clear in the last line of the texts from Isaiah, Paul, and John's gospel: "And I will heal him"; "And I will heal them". The Lord wills to heal us of our spiritual blindness and deafness, of the closedness of our heart, and of much more. He calls us to receive his healing, to be healed so that we may accept the graces of prayer that he has for us, so that we might move ahead in progress in prayer and in abiding in him.

Notes

[1] A good commentary is: E.W.T. Dicken, *The Crucible of Love. A Study of the Mysticism of St Teresa of Jesus and St John of the Cross* (London: Darton, Longman and Todd, 1963).

[2] London: Sheed and Ward, 1976.

[3] Trans. Paul Barrett (St Meinrad, Indiana: Abbey, 1974), pp. 31-86. The language refers often to persons as "souls" and to those in prayer of close union with God as "saints"; this could put off some people, in spite of the clarity and soundness of doctrine. See also three articles by Kevin O'Shea, C.SS.R.: "Enigma and Tenderness", *Spiritual Life*, 21 (1975), 137-152; "The Thorn and the Rose", *Spiritual Life*, 22 (1976), 86-95; "Littleness and Kindness", *Spiritual Life*, 23 (1977), 137-152.

[4] Francis A. Sullivan, "Baptism in the Holy Spirit", *Gregorianum*, 55 (1974), 49. This is the best theological study of the "baptism in the Spirit", and I rely on it here.

[5] *The Way of Perfection*, chapter 21.

Chapter Four
PRAYER AND INNER HEALING

Healing in response to prayer has been part of Christianity from the beginning. Recently a number of currents have converged to stimulate and renew interest in the healing power of God. In particular, the renewal of the healing sacraments, penance and the anointing of the sick, has focussed precisely on the healing power of the sacramental graces; and the charismatic renewal has witnessed a great many healings of all kinds.

Jesus as Healer
In the Gospel, Jesus heals. The saving power of God is present in Jesus to heal us, to save us; Jesus' healings reveal the divine work of our salvation, and they are part of that work. Jesus understands himself as a healer. In the synagogue, he reads Is 61:1-2, and applies it to himself: "The Spirit of the Lord is upon me, because he has anointed me to preach good news to the poor; he has sent me to proclaim release to the captives, and recovering of sight to the blind, to set free all who are oppressed" (Lk 4:18). When John's disciples ask Jesus who he is, he replies: "Go and tell John what you have seen and heard: the blind receive their sight, the lame walk, lepers are cleansed, the deaf hear, the dead are raised up . . ." (Lk 7:22).

Three kinds of healings appear in the Gospels. Jesus heals people spiritually; he forgives their sins and counsels them to change their lives; and following him they find themselves spiritually healed and their lives changed. Secondly, Jesus heals many people of what appear to us today as psychological problems. Among the many exorcisms, there seem to be some that are emotional or psychological cures rather than true exorcisms. At the time of Jesus' ministry, mankind had not yet discovered mental illness as a category of human behavior; it would have been normal for the Gospel writers to attribute psychoses and neuroses to the work of unclean or evil spirits. And, of course, Jesus heals many of physical diseases, even raising some from the dead.

All Jesus' healings are fruits of his compassion. He heals because he is God's saving and healing love present in the world. He has come as a doctor to minister to those who need healing (Mt 2:17).

In a mysterious way Jesus' death culminates his healing ministry, and "by his wounds we are healed" (Is 53:5; I Pet 2:24). "Just as Moses lifted up the serpent in the wilderness" to heal those bitten by snakes, "so the Son of Man must be lifted up that whoever believes may have eternal life in him" (Jn 3:14-15); "They shall look upon him whom they have pierced" (Jn 19:37; Zech 12:10); John's Gospel presents Jesus' death on the cross as a healing event. Matthew, Mark, and Luke include in the passion narrative the taunt, "He saved others; he cannot save himself"; the reference, of course, is to Jesus' healing ministry, and the irony is underlined — in his death, taunted, Jesus is a healer more than ever. The cross is the power of God (I Cor 1:17-18).

Jesus, after his death, continues to heal. He heals through his disciples in the Acts of the Apostles. Down through the centuries of christian history, the

47

Lord has healed through the saints, at shrines like Lourdes and Guadalupe, and through the sacraments. Actively present in his Church, the Lord still heals in answer to prayer.

Principles in Praying for Healing

Father Francis MacNutt, O.P., combining his training and experience as a theologian with what he has learned from his ministry of praying for healing, has written a basic book, *Healing,* that gives the theological principles and basic guidelines of prayer for healing.[1] In a later book, *The Power to Heal,* he shares discoveries and insights about praying for healing, especially for physical healing.[2] Father MacNutt acknowledges his debt to Agnes Sanford, a pioneer in teaching and writing about praying and healing.[3] Another well-known leader in the ministry of prayer for healing, Barbara Shlemon, has written *Healing Prayer.*[4] These authors teach rather than speculate; they encourage and counsel regarding prayer for healing, and they join reverence and sound theology with narrative examples of healings through prayer that come from their own experience.

Writers on praying for healing stress some fundamental points. The person that heals is Jesus, not the one doing the praying, and not the prayer. A theology professor once asked me what incantation I used to heal people. I had to tell him that I have never healed anyone, and that I do not use any incantation, because I am neither a magician nor a witch-doctor. The one that heals is the Lord. And he heals in answer to our prayers, not because we use magic and manipulate him — as though we could — or because we magically manipulate the forces of nature, but because he loves us and has compassion for us.

A second principle is this: faith counts. Books on healing in a religious context, including the best one, the New Testament, all underline the importance of praying with faith in the healing power of God. However, our faith is in the Lord, not in our faith; we believe in his love and power and we depend on that, not on our own faith. The fact that sometimes even persistent prayers for healing are not answered by healing does not mean that those prayers are without sufficient faith. As soon as we pray at all we enter the realm of the mystery of God's love and power, and we cannot have all the answers. We can only depend on God's goodness and accept reverently his answer to our prayers in whatever form he chooses it to take.

A third basic principle: the Lord certainly wants to heal us of whatever blocks our closer union with him. We cannot always know just what those blocks are. But we can pray for the healing of whatever we think might be holding us back in our union with the Lord, and we can pray with faith in the healing power of his love.

Spiritual Healing

The Samaritan woman, encountering Jesus at the well, experiences an interior healing (Jn 4:7-42). Jesus asks the woman for water. In answer, she teases him for stepping outside the bounds of social convention by speaking to her. Jesus then invites her with a double invitation: (1) to recognize him, and (2) to ask him for the living water. When she asks him for the living water, Jesus bring to the light the disorder in her life, past and present, and a reordering of the woman's life starts. She begins to recognize Jesus as the Messiah, and he responds by affirming her recognition. Converted, she uses her new freedom to announce the good news to other Samaritans.

The meeting between Jesus and the Samaritan woman describes the inner healing that takes place when we meet the Lord. He invites us to recognize him as Savior and to ask him for the living water, for his Spirit who guides and teaches us. The Lord reveals us to ourselves, bringing to the light of his healing love the past and present disorder in our lives. He converts us and heals us, and sends us to others in the new freedom that comes from accepting the living water.

In inner healing, we can distinguish spiritual healing and emotional (or psychological) healing. Of course, in us, the spiritual, the psychological, and the physical overlap and interpenetrate. We cannot separate them in practice. Spiritual healing always has a psychological component, and psychological healing will always include some spiritual healing and often also better physical health.

What is spiritual healing? It includes the grace of repentance, of forgiving others and of accepting God's forgiveness. It means a deeper conversion of heart and a closer adhesion to the Lord. Psychological healing depends to a great extent on repentance for sins and on the acceptance of God's forgiveness of those sins. This repentance and acceptance of God's mercy in reconciliation with him is a spiritual healing; it is closely connected to psychological healing and often leads to it. On the other hand, attachment to sin and unwillingness to repent and reform impedes psychological healing through the power of the Spirit.

The grace of repentance and of accepting reconciliation with God often depends on forgiving others. We can accept God's forgiveness only to the extent that we forgive others. And so we pray, "Forgive us our trespasses as we forgive those who trespass against us". When we fail to completely forgive those who have hurt us, the resentment or anger or hurt inside us keeps us from that openness to God that is necessary to receive his forgiveness. A heart partly closed to others means, necessarily, a heart partly closed to God.

Sometimes the failure to totally forgive remains unnoticed or even unconscious, below the surface of awareness; and so it is important to forgive others even when we think we already have forgiven, and even when those who hurt us meant us no harm and perhaps loved us greatly. Some of us need to forgive ourselves for our past sins, failures, mistakes, accepting Jesus' and the Father's total and unconditional acceptance of us and finding in their love the grace to accept ourselves. And some harbor partly buried anger against God for what he has permitted to happen; they need to drop their anger and accept his love without necessarily understanding his ways.

Psychological Healing

Often the Lord will work through some people to heal others, for example, through psychological counselling or through psychiatric help. In this way, personal prayer for psychological healing can reinforce, infuse, and make more fruitful regular individual or group therapy. A woman once complained to me that after two days of prayer for inner healing, nothing happened to her, although immediately afterward her sessions with her psychiatrist began to show considerable progress and her mental health improved rapidly through the therapy. I pointed out that the progress in her therapy was the answer to her prayer for inner healing.

On the other hand, the Lord does heal, both spiritually and psychologically, simply through prayer for inner healing. Much of what needs healing in us lies buried beneath the level of consciousness. Most of our psychological problems find their origins in anger, or in guilt feelings, or in fear, or in anxiety. And these in turn frequently result from root conflicts or hurts or wounds that remain unconscious and that go back to events we have partly or completely forgotten. We see, perhaps, only the tips of the icebergs that need to be melted. It helps to know what needs healing, but it is not necessary and is frequently difficult or impossible. We can pray to be healed interiorly insofar as we can recognize that we need healing, and then we can let the Lord guide us as to how to pray and what to pray for.

These mostly unconscious wounds and hurts come from the very beginning of our existence, from even before we were born. They come from our earliest months and years, from our childhood and growing up, from the whole process of living. They come from insufficient love and attention, from frightening or angering experiences, from humiliations. Some of them are contained in memories so deeply repressed we can never get at them. But the Lord sees all our hurts and can heal them.

One way to pray for inner healing is to pray for

healing of memories. I can ask the Lord to bring to my mind any past memory or memories that he wants to heal; and I can ask him to heal that memory — not to abolish it, but to take the hurt out of it, to take the fear or anger or guilt feelings out of it, and to change its meaning so that I can praise him for what happened to me. Memories to be healed might include memories of an alcoholic parent, or an overly strict or overly possessive parent; they can include memories of loneliness, being made fun of in school, of a serious accident, of physical abuse, of being misunderstood or not wanted or not trusted, and of hundreds of other things. I can bring these memories to the Lord's compassion for healing.

I can pray, too, for healing of my heart, of my affective drives. I can pray that the Lord heal my timidity, or my coldness of heart and inability to love and to accept love, or my fear of speaking in groups, or sadness or depression, or the roots of some sexual problem. These problems may have roots in unconscious memories, but the memories may be inaccessible; I can pray that the Lord heal what he sees needs healing.

And I can pray for greater freedom, for liberation from any habit or tendency that goes against progress in my union with God. I can pray that the Lord free me from selfishness, from fears, from undesirable behavior patterns, from sadness.

At the end of the day, when I come before the Lord to look at how I have walked with him during this past day, I may find some sins or faults or failures to love. I can hold those up to the Lord for forgiveness, and ask him to show me why I acted that way, from what roots the words or action sprang. And I can ask him to heal those roots, the

memory of the root of the problem, or the trouble-
some affective tendency in my heart; I can ask him
to free me from speaking or acting in that way, and
to free me from whatever bonds tie me and lie at the
source of my sin or fault or failure to love. The Lord
may show me, perhaps gradually over a period of
time, a whole web of sins and tendencies and
memories until, pulling on the web, he and I eventually come to the "spider" itself and eliminate it.
He may fill me with his love that casts out all fear
and anxiety, and let it sink into me, healing me. He
might take my resentment or hurt or guilt feelings,
and replace them with his forgiving love. He will,
certainly, somehow, answer my prayer.

Prayer and Inner Healing

The Lord will heal me through my union with him
in prayer simply because he came for that, to heal
me and to save me. I can cry out to him in confid-
ence; I can lament, I can complain to the Lord and
show him my wounds. Except for its liturgical use
of the Bible, and especially of the Psalms, Christianity has nearly lost the tradition of prayer of
lamentation. But lamentation is the cry to be
healed, to be set free, to be saved; it is the beginning
of healing, of freedom, of salvation.

Prayer of lament, common in the Old
Testament,[5] looks with hope to the future, to
healing, to liberation. It does not mourn or regret
in a backward look at past loss or failure; it cries out
to God for freedom; it is a lament not of mourning
but of affliction that expects healing. It appeals
directly to the Lord's compassion, showing him the
hurts, the anguish, the need for healing. Psalm 22,
which begins, "My God, my God, why have you

forsaken me?" is a prayer of lament. Psalm 102 prays, "Do not hide your face from me in the day of my distress!" Psalm 69 begins, "Save me, O God! The waters are up to my neck . . . my eyes grow dim with waiting for my God." Psalm 44 shouts, "Wake up! Why are you sleeping, Lord? Wake up!"

But the complaint always ends in hope, in trust in God's healing love and power.

> I wait for the Lord, my soul waits, and in
> his word I hope;
> My souls waits for the Lord more than
> watchmen for the morning, more than
> watchmen for the morning.
> O Israel, hope in the Lord.
>
> (Ps 130:3-7)

"And now Lord, what am I waiting for?" prays Psalm 39, "I put my hope in you" (verse 8). The hopefulness of the psalms of lament turns into prayers of petition for liberation, for salvation, and for healing. Psalm 22: "Hasten to my aid!" (verse 19), Psalm 69: "Let me be delivered from my enemies and from the deep waters" (verse 2). Psalm 88 appeals to God's goodness: "I spread out my hands to you . . . in the morning my prayer comes to you" (verses 9 and 13).

In the Gospels, the most common prayer of lament is the request to Jesus for healing. The Canaanite woman begs Jesus to heal her daughter (Mk 7:25-30). The ten lepers call out, "Jesus, Master, have mercy on us" (Lk 17:12-19). The blind beggar, Bartimaeus, shouts over and over, "Jesus, Son of David, have mercy on me" (Mk 10:46-52). A leper kneels before Jesus and says, "If you will, you

55

can make me clean" (Mk 1:40). Jesus encourages asking in faith, praying in the knowledge that if we ask we will receive, if we search we will find, if we knock, it will be opened to us. "And will not God vindicate his elect. who cry to him day and night? Will he delay long over them? I tell you, he will vindicate them speedily" (Lk 18:1-8).

Prayer, by its very nature as a personal relationship with the Lord, brings us into healing contact with the power of his love. His love recreates us, makes us grow, integrates us, knits up the frazzled parts into more of a wholeness. Hurt branches heal on the vine.

In the past few years, there have appeared several good books on inner healing. Francis MacNutt's *Healing* has two chapters on spiritual and emotional healing.[6] Matthew and Dennis Linn, two Jesuit priests who have a full-time healing ministry, have written *Healing of Memories: Prayer and Confession — Steps to Inner Healing,*[7] and *Healing Life's Hurts.*[8] The Linn brothers are especially helpful in giving step-by-step programs for personal prayer for inner healing. Ruth Stapleton has two recent books, *The Gift of Inner Healing,*[9] and *The Experience of Inner Healing.*[10] Father Michael Scanlan's books, *The Power in Penance,*[11] on inner healing as related to the sacrament of penance, and *Inner Healing,*[12] are especially useful to pastoral counselors in helping them to pray for inner healing with and for those who come to them for help.

Notes

[1] Notre Dame: Ave Maria, 1974. Another good book on praying for healing, informative, but not as practical, is Morton Kelsey, *Healing and Christianity* (New York: Harper,

1973).

[2] Notre Dame: Ave Maria, 1977.

[3] See, for example, her book, *The Healing Light* (Plainfield, N.J.: Logos, 1947).

[4] Notre Dame: Ave Maria, 1976.

[5] See, for example, Ps 22, 39, 42, 44, 51, 60, 74, 79, 80, 102, 130, 140, 142; Deut 26:5-10; Gen 21:16-20; Judg 21:2; II Chron 6:24-31.

[6] *Op. cit.,* pp. 169-191.

[7] New York: Paulist, 1974.

[8] New York: Paulist, 1978.

[9] Waco: Word, 1976.

[10] Waco: Word, 1977.

[11] New York: Paulist, 1972.

[12] New York: Paulist, 1974.

II. CONTEMPORARY VOICES

"In prayer, we discover what we already have . . . Everything has been given us in Christ. All we need is to experience what we already possess." (Thomas Merton)

"Christ, his Heart, a Fire, capable of penetrating everything – and which, little by little, spreads everywhere." (Pierre Teilhard de Chardin)

"Jesus Christ gives the unity to scripture . . . It is he and he alone who explains it to us, and in explaining it, he explains himself." (Henri de Lubac)

Chapter Five

THOMAS MERTON: SOLITUDE AND THE TRUE SELF

Thomas Merton, one of the few great theologians of this century, has prayer as the center and central theme — almost the only theme — of his theology. He describes prayer briefly as "a consciousness of one's union with God",[1] and "an awareness of one's inner self".[2] Merton understands these two as synonomous. My true inner self is my self as united with God. In finding my true self, I find my-self-in-union-with-God. To pray is to do this consciously. To pray, to find God by finding my true self, I need solitude; and in prayerful solitude I find not only God and myself but the world and all in it, not as it sees itself but as it stands in reality.

The enormous volume of Merton's writings, over sixty books and hundreds of articles, extending from the 1948 publication of the autobiographical *The Seven Storey Mountain* to his accidental death in 1968, reflect the search that formed his life: the search for God, for himself in God, and for solitude. The search for union with God led Thomas Merton, from the time of his conversion to Roman Catholicism and through his years as a Trappist monk, to look for always more complete solitude; as he increasingly found it, his understanding of it developed.[3] He came to appreciate solitude less as a somewhat harsh exterior flight from the world and its concerns, and more as an interior silence, a state of the heart, in which he found a new compassion for all God's creatures and a renewed concern for the world's problems.

After graduating from Columbia University and becoming a Catholic, Merton taught for a year at Saint Bonaventure University, run by the Franciscan Order. There, he thought seriously about becoming either a Franciscan or a Trappist; one day, considering his future, he opened his Bible on impulse and read the angel's words to Zachariah, "Behold, you will be silent" (Lk 1:20). To Merton the words meant that God seemed to call him to the silent life of a Trappist monk.[4] The conviction grew, and in late 1941 he arrived at Gethsemani monastery in Kentucky to look for God in solitude.

While there, he wrote in his journal, "I have only one desire, and that is the desire for solitude – to disappear into God."[5] He added later, "It is clear to me that solitude is my vocation, not as a flight from the world, but as my place in the world."[6]

Merton's call to solitude caused him problems. The Carthusian Order attracted Merton because of its austere solitary life and, although he later called that attraction a temptation that made him a nuisance to his spiritual directors,[7] it began a long series of temptations to leave the Trappists for greater aloneness with God. Merton's struggle with these temptations manifested an authentic call to sink deeper into the silence of God, a call that led him gradually to greater physical solitude within his own religious order. Finally, at the age of fifty, Merton received his superiors' permission to live as a full time hermit on the monastery grounds at Gethsemani.

But the search for solitude continued. Three years later, looking for still greater possibilities for a solitary life, Merton accepted an invitation to speak at an ecumenical conference of Asian monastic leaders in Bangkok, Thailand, stopping on the way in California and in Alaska to give talks and to look for still greater possibilities for solitude. He considered moving to a more isolated hermitage, retaining his identity as a monk of Gethsemani but living even more completely alone, far from his monastery. In Bangkok, December 10, 1968, alone in his room, Thomas Merton touched a large fan after taking a shower and, electrocuted, died instantly. He had written earlier, "Every man is a solitary, held firmly by the inexorable limitations of his aloneness. Death makes this very clear, for when a man dies, he dies alone.[8]

Solitude

In Thomas Merton's spiritual teaching, some physical solitude, exterior silence, and real recollection are necessary for anyone who wants to have a serious prayer life. But they are means to an end. Solitude is not an end in itself, as though shutting myself off from the world, stuffing myself inside my own mind and closing the door like a turtle could have value.[9] The purpose that exterior solitude serves is not isolation but communion. We "go into the desert" for love of God and to enter into deeper communion with him; this is the primary purpose of physical solitude whether for an hour of prayer or a lifetime of living as a hermit. The secondary purpose regards other people; we go "into the desert" not to escape them but to learn how to find them, not to get rid of being responsible for them, but to find out how to help them the most.[10]

Everyone, then, needs some physical solitude in order to have a serious prayer life, but only because it is a condition for *interior* solitude, which is more fundamental and more important. "There is no true solitude except interior solitude."[11] True solitude is not an absence of people or of noise around me; it is an abyss opening up in the center of my soul.[12] And I need interior solitude in order to find my true self, in order to find myself as a person. To be a person is to have an incommunicable inner solitude, and to discover my inner solitude is to begin to discover my own true identity. Merton stresses the need for solitude as found in the very essence of being a person; "It is at once our loneliness and our dignity to have an incommunicable personality that is ours, ours alone and no one else's, and will be so forever."[13]

For this reason, "solitude is as necessary for society as silence is for language and air for the lungs and food for the body."[14] Any society needs to provide sufficient solitude to develop the inner life of the persons who form that society. And if it does not, many will seek a false solitude – self-centered, proud, separatist, aloof but needing to manipulate others. Just as the christian hermit, living apart from others, loving them, one with them, symbolizes the true solitude to which in some ways God calls all of us; so too the dictator stands for that false solitude that, in the midst of others, consumes them violently to fill its own emptiness.[15]

Contemporary society does not put a high value on any kind of solitude. The "gregarious illusion", the "sheep mentality", dominates society today.[16] In totalitarian societies, mass movements provide an ersatz identity, and escape from freedom, "a renunciation of personal responsibility in order to live not by one's own mind and one's own freedom but by the thought and decisions of the group: the party line, the will of the leader."[17] Modern democratic societies impose the same conformist pressures, but in more subtle ways, and encourage us "to forget and to exorcise that solitude which seems to be a demon."[18]

"Mass man", "collectivist man", lives in a state of alienation. Merton uses the basically Marxist notion of alienation, adapting it to his own purposes. What alienation means "is that man living under certain conditions is no longer in possession of the fruits of his life. His life is not his. His life is lived according to conditions determined by someone else."[19] Caught up in the norms of collectivist society, I can believe that the exterior and superficial self that society gives me is the real me. It is not; it is a false self, a wrong identity.

With no solitude and no silence, I lose my self, become alienated from my true self, and so too from God and from others, and even from nature. In solitude, I can, with God's grace, overcome my alienation. I can let my false self crack and crumble off, and I can painfully discover in the silence of God who I really am. "The Lord is watching in the almond trees, over the fulfillment of his words", writes Merton, referring to Jeremiah 1:11, and he adds that whether there is noise or not, whether there be voices in the field or not, whether the radio is going or silent, whether the house is full of children or empty, "the almond tree brings forth her fruit in silence."[20]

The True Self

Merton distinguishes between the true self and the false self. In his last, most mature, and perhaps best book, *Contemplative Prayer,* he writes:

> The way of prayer brings us face to face with the sham and the false self that seeks to live for itself alone and to enjoy the "consolation of prayer" for its own sake. This "self" is pure illusion, and ultimately he who lives for and by such an illusion must end either in disgust or in madness.[21]

"Our external everyday self is to a great extent a mask and a fabrication."[22] The false self is that "self" that tries to live independently of God, that wants to center on itself rather than to go out of itself in love; it is the narcissistic self that "is at best an impostor and a stranger."[23]

> Everyone of us is shadowed by an illusory person: a false self . . . the man that I want myself to be but who cannot exist, because God does not know anything about him. And to be unknown of God is altogether too much privacy. My false and private self is the one who wants to exist outside the reach of God's will and God's love . . . And such a self cannot help but be an illusion.[24]

My true self, not easy to find, lies hidden in obscurity at my center where I depend directly on God. My prayer, then, should begin with the realization of my helplessness in the presence of God and of my utter dependence on him. Then I will know God in prayer through my loving union with him, not as I might know an object but with a different kind of knowledge in which I seem to disappear into God, to know him alone, not to know myself apart from him.[25]

What is my true self? "Who am I?" Merton asked in a talk he gave. "My deepest realization of who I am is — I am one loved by Christ . . . The depths of my identity are in the center of my being where I am known by God."[26] My deep self is hidden with Christ in God, and unless I discover this true self, I will never really know myself, nor will I know God. "For it is by the door of this deep self that we enter into the spiritual knowledge of God."[27]

In the flight from the "obligation to *love*", western culture has fallen into an individualism in which the person seems an isolated unit, lost, identifiable only by his separation from all the other units.[28] For Merton, the process of self-realization, of finding and becoming more my true self, lies not in separation but in union of love. Self-realization takes place in the growing awareness that I am truly quite different from my ordinary self-centered self. It is more "natural" for me to "go out of myself" and be carried freely towards God, in himself or in others, than to be centered and closed in on myself.[29]

That I am to some extent alienated from the world, from other people, and from my true self, depends on my alienation from God. To overcome these alienations, I must move more toward my true self, the self that is related to all other people and to God. I must enter deeply into myself and, passing through the center of myself, go out of myself into God. I must renounce my false self, my superficial external self, to find within myself my true self, the true "I" who is united to God in Jesus Christ.[30] Becoming radically poor, giving up all the inordinate needs that my false self clamors to fulfill, I grow in the capacity to surrender myself to God. Emptying myself of the contents of the false self, I find myself as made in the image and likeness of God. In losing my false self for the sake of Jesus Christ, I find my true self hidden in him. "It is this inner self," Merton writes, "that is taken up into the mystery of Christ, by his love, by the Holy Spirit, so that in secret we live in Christ."[31]

Contemplative Prayer

Prayer, then, consists of becoming aware, in a loving way, of my true self, of who I really am. And my true self is myself in union with God present in Jesus Christ. With an inner solitude, in an interior silence even though I find myself in a noisy world, I quietly let my true self, the "I" in a love relationship in Christ with God, emerge. So, losing myself in solitude, I find my self, and I find God. And, finding him, I find everything in him. This is prayer.

I am already united with God through my incorporation into Christ through baptism; and through grace the Holy Spirit lives in my heart, and Jesus and the Father have their dwelling with me. My union with God already exists. Prayer is a becoming conscious of this union, *"a conscious realization of the union that is already truly effected"* between my soul and God by grace.[32] Many people, Merton observes, "have a special attraction to the presence of God within them, or to some other form of consciousness of God's nearness to their intimate being." This grace, though quite normal, is not shared by all. But even persons who do not have this attraction should realize that the purpose of their prayer "is to bring them somehow into conscious communion with the God who is the source" of all the life and the goodness within them.[33]

The real purpose of prayer, in Merton's view, both of personal prayer in private and of prayer in the Christian assembly, is the deepening of the awareness of God, the deepening of personal realization in love. "even if sometimes this awareness may amount to a negative factor, a seeming 'absence' ".[34] In a talk given just before he left for Bangkok, Merton put the matter simply:

> In prayer we discover what we already have. You start where you are, you deepen what you already have, and you realize that you are already there. We already have everything, but we don't know it and we don't experience it. Everything has been given to us in Christ. All we need is to experience what we already possess.[35]

And the talk continues:

> The whole thing boils down to giving ourselves in prayer a chance to realize that we have what we seek. We don't have to rush after it. It is there all the time, and if we give it time, it will make itself known to us.[36]

This kind of prayer Merton calls contemplative prayer. He does not restrict the word "contemplative" to higher realms of prayer. All prayer should, in some way, have a contemplative perspective because all prayer is communion with God, and because contemplation gives life to religion. "Without contemplation, liturgy tends to be a mere pious show", and prayer outside the liturgy becomes "plain babbling". Not everyone can become a contemplative monk, but "that is not the point; what matters is the *contemplative orientation* of the whole life of prayer.[37] Without this contemplative orientation our apostolate is more for our own glory than for the glory of God, our preaching becomes mere proselytizing to ensure universal conformity with our own way of life, and the Church is reduced to being "the servant of cynical and worldly powers."[38] Without true and deep contemplative aspirations, religion tends in the end to become "the opium of the people".[39]

Contemplative prayer takes the presence of the Holy Spirit seriously. Its purpose is to bring his presence into awareness,

> . . . and to bring our hearts into harmony with his voice, so that we allow the Holy Spirit to speak and to pray within us, and to lend him our voices and our affections that we may become, as far as possible, conscious of his prayer in our hearts.[40]

For it is the Holy Spirit "who teaches us to pray, and who, though we do not always know how to pray as we ought, prays in us, and cries out to the Father in us."[41]

But is the christian life of prayer, with its contemplative orientation, just an evasion of the real problems, an escape from the conflicts and anxieties of existence today? Merton answers that "if we pray in the Spirit, we are certainly not running away from life . . . for the Spirit of the Lord has filled the whole earth."[42] Prayer does not remove us from the world; it gives us a rock to stand on in the sea of the world, and it teaches us to swim securely in the world's waters. In his last talk before he died, Merton said:

> You can't just immerse yourself in the world and get carried away with it. That is no salvation. If you want to pull a drowning man out of the water, you have to have some support yourself. Supposing somebody is drowning and you are standing on a rock, you can do it; or supposing you can support yourself by swimming, you can do it. There is nothing to be gained by simply jumping in the water and drowning with him.[43]

Prayer does not shut us off from the world, blinding us to its hard realities; it transforms our vision of the world and lets us see it, and all mankind and all history, in the light of God.[44]

Contemplation opens us up to the world we live in, to the world as the place of the revelation of God "as Judge and as Savior, as the Lord of history",[45] to the world with its critical problems which are basically spiritual, to the world of the people that the Lord in one way or another brings to us that we might help them.[46] Contemplation

71

gives us perspective on the world, clear vision with compassion and above all with hope — for the Lord is risen and is with us. It makes us see that the world has "a transcendent and personal center, . . . the risen and deathless Christ in whom all are fulfilled in One".[47]

> As if we had forgotten how the whips
>   of winter
> And the cross of April
> Would all be lost in one bright miracle.
> For look! The vine on Calvary is bright
>   with branches![48]

Notes

[1] *Spiritual Direction and Meditation* (Collegeville: Liturgical Press, 1960), p. 67.

[2] "Conference on Prayer", taped recording, quoted in John J. Higgins, *Merton's Theology of Prayer* (Spencer: Cistercian Publications, 1971), p. xix.

[3] The sketchy analysis in this chapter of Merton's idea of solitude is based partly on a doctoral thesis, so far unpublished, by Richard Cashen, C.P., *The Concept of Solitude in the Thought of Thomas Merton* (Rome: Pontifical Gregorian University, 1976). See the very interesting article of Sister Therese Lentfoehr, "Thomas Merton: the Dimensions of Solitude", *The American Benedictine Review*, 23 (1972), 337-352.

[4] *The Seven Storey Mountain* (New York: Signet Books, 1948), pp. 326-327.

[5] *The Sign of Jonas* (New York: Doubleday Image, 1956), p. 26.

[6] *Ibid.*, p. 251.

[7] *Ibid.*, p. 13.

[8] *Disputed Questions* (New York: Farrar, Strauss, and Cudahy, 1960), pp. 180-181.

[9] *New Seeds of Contemplation* (Norfolk, Connecticut: New Directions, 1961), p. 34.

[10] *Ibid.*, p. 80.

[11] *Seeds of Contemplation* (Norfolk, Connecticut: New Directions, 1949), p. 42.

[12] *New Seeds of Contemplation, op. cit.*, p. 80.

[13] *No Man Is an Island* (New York: Doubleday Image, 1967), p. 184.

[14] *Ibid.*, p. 185.

[15] *Ibid.*, pp. 185-186.

[16] *Ibid.*, p. 11.

[17] *Disputed Questions, op. cit.*, p. 135.

[18] *Ibid.*, p. 183.

[19] "Marxist Theory and Monastic Theoria", quoted in J. Higgins, *op. cit.*, p. 41, note 48.

[20] *No Man Is an Island, op. cit.*, p. 192.

[21] *Contemplative Prayer* (New York: Doubleday Image, 1971), p. 24.

[22] *Ibid.*, p. 70.

[23] *The New Man* (New York: Mentor-Omega Books, 1961), p. 73.

[24] *New Seeds of Contemplation, op. cit.*, p. 34.

[25] *Contemplative Prayer, op. cit.*, pp. 75-76.

[26] "A Conference on Prayer", *Sisters Today*, 41 (1970), 452.

[27] *The New Man, op. cit.*, p. 75.

[28] *Disputed Questions, op. cit.*, p. ix.

[29] *The New Man, op. cit.*, p. 77.

[30] *New Seeds of Contemplation, op. cit.*, p. 7; "Notes on Contemplation", *Spiritual Life*, 7 (1961), 200.

[31] *New Seeds of Contemplation, op. cit.*, p. 259.

[32] *Spiritual Direction and Meditation, op. cit.*, p. 67.

[33] *Ibid.*, p. 67.

[34] *Contemplation in a World of Action* (London: Allen and Unwin, 1971), p. 164.

[35] David Steindl-Rast, "Recollections of Thomas Merton's Last Days in the West", *Monastic Studies*, 7 (1969), 2-3.

[36] *Ibid.*, p. 3.

[37] *Contemplative Prayer, op. cit.*, p. 114.

[38] *Ibid.*, pp. 115-116.

[39] *Ibid.*, p. 113.

[40] *Spiritual Direction and Meditation, op. cit.*, p. 79.

[41] *Ibid.*, p. 78.

[42] *Contemplative Prayer, op. cit.*, p. 112.

[43] *The Asian Journal of Thomas Merton*, ed. N. Burton *et al.* (New York: New Directions, 1975), p. 341.

[44] *Contemplative Prayer, op. cit.*, p. 112.

[45] *Contemplation in a World of Action, op. cit.*, p. 136.

[46] *Ibid.*, pp. 138-139.

[47] *Mystics and Zen Masters* (New York: Farrar, Strauss, and Giroux, 1967), p. 42.

[48] From Merton's poem, "The Vine"; I do not have access to the American edition of this poem, but found it in *Poesie*, ed. A. Guidi (Brescia: Morcelliana, 1952), p. 12, an edition of fourteen of Merton's poems in English and Italian parallel texts.

Chapter Six

PIERRE TEILHARD DE CHARDIN: THE WORLD AND THE RISEN CHRIST

When the Jesuit scientist Pierre Teilhard de Chardin fell dead of a heart attack on Easter Sunday, 1955, he left stacks of unedited writings. Although during his lifetime he was misunderstood by the Church and forbidden by his superiors to publish anything religious, Teilhard's influence since his death has been enormous. His ideas permeate the documents of the Second Vatican Council, and especially the statement that time has proved the most important, on the Church in the Modern World. His vision, circulated in mimeographed and carbon copies before his death, helped form a generation of European theologians and lies behind much contemporary theology of sin and redemption, of liberation, of the Church, and of the full humanity of Jesus Christ.

His religious writings, the most important of them published only in the last few years, have given rise to serious study and to innumerable doctoral dissertations. They show in their totality that Teilhard's thought is centered on the person of Jesus Christ risen. They do not indicate the great extent to which his written thought issued from his lived experience and particularly from his prayer.

Not long ago I set out to find the notebooks in which Teilhard de Chardin kept the notes on his prayer from his annual eight-day retreats. I found them in the custody of the Jesuits at Chantilly, just north of Paris, locked carefully in a desk drawer, completely unavailable to the eyes even of researchers. I studied the notebooks scrupulously over a period of several days, and discovered that the source of Teilhard's ideas and the fire they were forged in was his prayer. His thought came from his prayer, and he prayed through it before he put it into essay and book form.

Unlike Thomas Merton, Teilhard de Chardin has no explicit theology of prayer. But all his religious writings grew out of his prayer and were refined in it. In fact, some of his early essays are written as prayers. "The Mass on the World",[1] for example, is the prayer he composed and used when he found himself on geological expeditions in China and unable to say Mass. When Teilhard described in the third person and in poetic fiction form three mystical experiences of the loving presence of the risen Jesus in today's world, he was in fact describing his own mystical experiences.[2] The prayers contained in his spiritual classic *The Divine Milieu*[3] are products of his personal prayer.

Personal Relationship with Jesus Christ Risen

According to Teilhard the central religious problem of western culture today is what he calls "the problem of the two faiths".[4] The average Christian wants to give himself to God, has faith in God, lives in at least some awareness of the spiritual and transcendent, and looks upward to God for the fundamental meaning of his life. This vertical vector in christian life enters into apparent conflict with a horizontal and forward impulse: to give oneself to the world, to one's family and friends and work, to building up the world around one. The Christian today has faith in the world as well as faith in God. But these two faiths seem in opposition, at least to some extent.

Furthermore, our faith in the world and its future grows gradually weaker, undermined by the failures of human society to solve its problems, by economic, social, political, and environmental setbacks, by wars and revolutions, by the oppression of human rights, and by the abuse of scientific and technological advances. Personal problems, failures, misunderstandings, can further eat away our faith in the future and leave us hurt and less trusting. Faith in the world is in crisis. And so is christian faith in God. They need each other; they are mutually complementary.

Christian faith remains incomplete as long as it does not take the Incarnation of God in Jesus Christ seriously. It becomes rigid, legalistic, less human because out of contact with lived human reality; it becomes too small, limiting and repressive, closed in on itself, "other-worldly", un-christian. God does not hold himself aloof from the world. In Jesus, he has taken on our humanity.

God has descended into the world in Jesus Christ, who entered even further into the heart of the world through his death on the cross (Phil 2:6-11) so that, risen, he might be the heart of the world. God has, in Jesus, entered into a kind of mutuality with our world. Christ's resurrection does not take him out of the world so much as it enables him to transcend it and so to envelop it with his universal loving presence and influence. The world exists, holds together, in the risen Christ (Col 1:15-20) and moves forward in the direction of the final reconciliation of all things in Christ at the end of time (Eph 1:9-10). Teilhard puts Paul's understanding of Jesus risen, the personal and transcendent Center of the world in whom all things exist and will be reconciled, into an evolutionary perspective. Christ risen, for Teilhard, is the future focal point of all true progress, of the world, of human society, and of each person

Because Jesus stands risen at the end of history, at the end of the world's history and at the end of the personal history in this world of each of us, because by drawing all things to himself by the influence of his love he makes history go, moves it forward toward himself, he gives us hope. The future has a face, the face of the glorified Christ; we can have faith in the world and in the future because we have faith in Jesus as the Lord of history. Faith in God and faith in the world are drawn into synthesis in one faith in Jesus Christ. The God of the "upward" is the God of the "forward". The vertical and the horizontal components of christian existence come together in the Christian's personal faith relationship with Jesus Christ.

Teilhard de Chardin gives us a better understanding of how prayer can integrate our lives. The Jesus to whom I pray is the risen Lord and the personal center of the world and its future — and so of my world and my future. Nothing is irrelevant to my relationship with him; nothing is excluded, because he is the center of everything. And my relation to the Lord in prayer is one of hope; I can give him my fears and worries about the present and the future because he holds both in his hands. Prayer does not take me out of the world. On the contrary, it brings me more consciously into union with the risen Jesus who stands at its center. I am never more truly *in* the world (though not *of* the world), never more fully involved in the world, than when praying; because then I enter into conscious communion with the world's Center.[5]

Union in Love

One of the fundamental principles of Teilhard de Chardin's thought is that "union differentiates".[6] Union does not suffocate or confuse the elements united; it differentiates them within the unity. In any area of life, whether we refer to the cells of a body or the members of a team, union differentiates the elements united. For example, on a basketball team, players are, within the team unity, differentiated according to their playing positions; on a surgical team different members have different functions. Good teamwork goes together with a high degree of specialization.

When the union is primarily a union of love (and not primarily functional, as winning basketball games, or performing an operation), then the persons are differentiated precisely as persons: they are "personalized", grow as persons, become more "person". Sometimes we do not see that union of love personalizes because we confuse "person" with "individual". We find our true selves as persons not by isolating ourselves as individuals but by uniting with others as persons. In close friendships, when they are well ordered and unselfish, the friends grow as persons through the friendship. In a marriage based on love and sacrifice, the married persons grow as persons not in spite of their daily lived out marriage union but because of it; they bring out the

79

best in each other.

What is essential for a union to be personalizing is that it be a union of love, "center to center, through internal attraction".[7] True union is a union of love, for "love is what brings persons together not superficially and tangentially, but center to center."[8]

The most sublime illustration of Teilhard's principle that union of love personalizes is the Trinity. Jesus, the Father, and the Holy Spirit share, in an infinitely intimate union, the one divine nature. At the same time, the three divine Persons are infinitely distinct. No persons could be more united or more "persons". When I am united with the Trinity, I am caught up into an infinitely loving community. The Holy Spirit, whose name is Love, in uniting me to himself, makes himself the principle of my life and personal growth. Union with the Holy Spirit, and in the Spirit with the Father and with Jesus, is the mainspring of my development and of my fulfillment as a person.

Prayer, then, as the entering consciously into this union with Jesus and the Father in the Holy Spirit, is the most important activity of christian personalization. In conscious personal relationship with Jesus Christ, in his Spirit, and through Christ with the Father, I grow through loving and being loved; I grow as a person, become more myself, more the person God has always intended me to be. Remaining consciously in Jesus I grow, just as branches grow on a vine.

The Heart of Jesus

Teilhard de Chardin's own personal prayer, as can be seen from his letters, from his personal journals, and especially in his private retreat notes, was usually to

Jesus Christ as risen and glorified. This personal relationship with Christ had its origin in the personal attachment to the heart of Jesus that his mother had taught him and that never left him. And Teilhard's theology of the risen Christ as the future focal center of the converging history of the world has its roots in this same attachment. In his private journal of 1919, Teilhard writes that, although he had never really analyzed it before, the conjunction of God and the world has taken place in the heart of Christ. "There lies the power", he writes, "that from the beginning has attracted me and conquered me; . . . all the later development of my interior life has been nothing other than *the evolution of that seed.*"[9]

In his 1939 retreat, eight days of prayerful solitude, Teilhard wrote on the seventh day:

> First Friday (December 1, 1939)
> The Sacred Heart: Instinctively and mysteriously for me, since my infancy: the *synthesis* of Love and Matter, of Person and Energy. From this there has gradually evolved in me the perception Christ uniting all things in a universal cohesion. I would like to spread this vision (I do not want to say "devotion", much too sentimental and too weak) of the universal Christ, of the *true* heart of Jesus.[10]

The notes of his other retreats contain frequent references to the heart of Jesus. "The Sacred Heart", he writes on the first day of his 1943 retreat, "is the Center of Christ, who centers all on himself."[11]

Teilhard's attachment to the heart of Jesus had none of the sentimental narrowness often found in the traditional devotion that began in seventeenth-century France. On the contrary, it freed him because it enabled him to find a unity and a consistency in all of reality, because it showed him the absolute Center of a changing world. Through the symbol of Jesus' heart the Divine took on for Teilhard the properties, the form, and the qualities of a Fire capable of transforming anything and everything through the power of its love. "Christ, his Heart, a Fire, capable of penetrating everything — and which, little by little, spreads everywhere."[12]

Judging from Teilhard's journals and retreat notes, his prayer, at least in the second half of his life, was dominated more by darkness than by light. Intellectually, he saw the heart of Jesus as a burning flame; in his prayer it was a rock to hang on to in the dark. All his adult life he had a feeling of anguish.[13] Teilhard's strong hope in Christ's coming a second time and in the value of our building the world toward his coming, his complete trust in the love of Christ for him and for the world around him, did not eliminate the fear of death in his later years, nor the attacks of anxiety that came more frequently as he grew older, nor the darkness of his prayer.

"So there are two anxieties regarding death", he writes in the notes of his 1939 retreat, "(1) will Jesus be there?, (2) will he take me with him or will he reject me?"[14] And in 1943, "The big question and the initial hesitation: Is the divine Center imaginary? Man, does he not stand alone? Answer: the Christian *sees through* the coming future (God is Love *now)* in the light of the revelation of

Christ."[15] He writes of his difficulty in accepting old age, "a life without a future for oneself — face to the wall."[16] A few years later, in a public debate with Gabriel Marcel, he states — as against the views expressed by Marcel — that we must throw ourselves into building the world, trying every avenue, and that this will not lead us to a Promethean pride for "we will feel our weakness more and depend on God more."[17] Teilhard did feel his weakness, all his life, but especially as he grew older. That the darkness did not diminish his faith but rather strengthened it tells us something about prayer.

Notes

[1] "Christ in the World of Matter" in *Hymn of the Universe*, trans. S. Bartholomew (New York: Harper and Row, 1965), pp. 41-55.

[2] In *ibid.*, conversation with Mlle. Jeanne Mortier, Teilhard's secretary for many years; Paris, summer, 1973.

[3] Trans. B. Wall *et al.* (New York: Harper and Row, 1960); see, on Teilhard's spiritual doctrine, H. de Lubac, *The Religion of Teilhard de Chardin* (New York: Desclee, 1967), especially Chapter Two, pp. 20-27.

[4] See especially "The Heart of the Problem", in *The Future of Man*, trans. N. Denny (New York: Harper and Row, 1964), pp. 260-269.

[5] By "world" here, I mean not the world as under God's judgment, the world of sin and regression from God, but the world that moves toward the final reconciliation of all in it in Christ, the world that God so loves that he sent his only Son to save it. For a theology of involvement in the world based on Teilhard's ideas, see R. Faricy, *Building God's World* (Denville, N.J.: Dimension, 1976).

[6] Teilhard's fullest explanation of this principle can be found in "The Grand Option", in *The Future of Man, op. cit.*, pp. 52-57. See also: "The Formation of the Noosphere", in *ibid.*, pp. 182-184; *Man's Place in Nature*, trans. R. Hague (New York: Harper and Row, 1966), pp. 114-115; "My Universe", in *Science and Christ*, trans. R. Hague (New York:

Harper and Row), pp. 45-46; R. Faricy, *Teilhard de Chardin's Theology of the Christian in the World* (New York: Sheed and Ward, 1967), pp. 59-63.

[7] "Life and the Planets", in *The Future of Man, op. cit.*, p. 263.

[8] "The Direction and Conditions of the Future", in *ibid.*, p. 235.

[9] *Cahier* F, October 17, 1919, quoted by P. Schellenbaum, *Le Christ dans l'énergétique Teilhardienne* (Paris: Editions du Cerf, 1971), p. 192.

[10] Unpublished retreat notes, 1939-1943.

[11] *Ibid.*

[12] "Le Coeur de la matiere", in *Le Coeur de la matière,* vol. 13 of the *Oeuvres de Pierre Teilhard de Chardin* (Paris: Editions du Seuil, 1976), p. 21.

[13] Interview with Claude Cuenot, December 4, 1968, quoted in: Hugh Campbell Cairns, *The Identity and Originality of Teilhard* (unpublished doctoral dissertation presented at the University of Edinburgh, March 30, 1971), p. 477.

[14] Unpublished retreat notes, 1939-1943.

[15] *Ibid.*

[16] Unpublished retreat notes, 1944-1954.

[17] Unpublished notes from the debate held January 21, 1949, Paris, pp. 3-4, in the files of the *Fondation Teilhard de Chardin*, Paris.

Chapter Seven
HENRI DE LUBAC: SCRIPTURE'S MEANING FOR PRAYER

Henri de Lubac, the French Jesuit whose first book, *Catholicism,*[1] set the agenda in 1938 for Roman Catholic theological renewal right up to the Second Vatican Council, has had an even greater influence on theology during and after the Council. His momumental contribution to christian thought consists chiefly in uncovering traditional areas of christian reflection that have been overlooked and neglected in this age. He has sometimes seemed revolutionary because in his efforts to stress Christianity's equilibrium by restoring essential points to its attention, he has often had to go against modern currents. What he writes is new because nearly everyone else has forgotten it. His theological perspectives, historical and traditionalist, have repeatedly broken through a rigid theological *status quo* to renew theology and to give it in a fuller way its ancient balance. The examples are too numerous to list. They include his studies of the relationships between nature and grace and between the Church and the Eucharist, of the social nature of salvation, of the traditionalism of Teilhard de Chardin's contemporary religious intuitions, and of the spiritual interpretation of scripture.[2]

The Spiritual Interpretation of Scripture

In studying scripture in order to learn its first or literal meaning, what the words say, I shine the light of my reason (enlightened by faith) and my acquired knowledge and skills upon the written word so as to illuminate its meaning. In the spiritual interpretation of scripture, on the other hand, I let the scripture shine on me, to illuminate the christian beliefs I hold, to throw light on myself and my situation now in the world, and to shed its rays on my future hidden in God.

The spiritual meaning of scripture, then, is the meaning I find when I prayerfully apply scripture to myself and my situation. It is a faith-reading of scripture that considers the inspired word of God as addressed to me here and now; I read God's word prayerfully and I hear him speak that word directly to me. Reading scripture for its spiritual meaning is a way of entering into dialogue with the Lord – a way of praying.

In other words, one way to use scripture in prayer is to take it according to its literal meaning – what the author intended to communicate – and let the light shine from that; that light is the spiritual meaning. I "take scripture as a lamp for lighting a way through the dark until the dawn comes and the morning star rises" in my understanding (II Peter 1:19).

The Cistercian abbot André Louf has put it this way:

> Not only is the spiritual reading of the Bible not identified with its scientific study, but one might even say in a certain sense it goes in the opposite direction.

> Scientific study reconstructs the past . . .
> The Christian with faith listens day by
> day to what the Eternal Word wants to
> make known to him here and now from
> the past, . . . clarified by the efforts of
> biblical science.[3]

"In sacred scripture", Henri de Lubac writes, "there are basically only two meanings, the literal meaning and the spiritual meaning, and they are not in opposition but in continuity."[4] "They are related to one another in the way that the Old and the New Testaments are related; more precisely, they constitute — they *are* — the Old and the New Testaments."[5] That is, the letter of the Old Testament has a spiritual meaning that points directly or indirectly to Jesus, and until we see that fact we do not really understand the Old Testament. The traditional symbols of this relationship between the two parts of the Bible and the two Covenants (the word "testament" means both the "old" or "new" part of the Bible, and also "covenant") are the changing of the water to wine at Cana, and the Transfiguration. The water of the Old Testament is turned into the wine of the New. On the mountain, the Old Covenant, represented by Moses and Elias, supports the New; only the New remains: "And they saw only Jesus." This idea is clearly worked out as early as Origen, and later develops into the doctrine of "the four meanings of scripture".

De Lubac holds that the four senses of the Bible are already implicit in Origen; they become explicit and widely referred to especially in the Middle Ages. The first is the *literal* meaning: what the text means to say, its first meaning, the sense expressed by the words themselves in their total context. The other three senses are sub-divisions of the spiritual sense, kinds of spiritual meaning.

Doctrine, Life, and the Life to Come

The *allegorical* meaning of scripture sees things in the Old Testament as figures of Christ or of the Church or of both at the same time. The people of Israel prefigure both Jesus and the Church, as does the Jerusalem temple. The Passover is a type of the crucifixion, and the celebration of Passover is a type of the Last Supper. Adam, Moses, David, Jeremiah prefigure Jesus. The allegorical sense of a given text or part of the Bible expresses the christian faith regarding Jesus and the Church; it teaches christian doctrine, the mysteries of the faith. The Old Testament, allegorically, points to the mystery of Christ, and it contains that mystery as its inner meaning. It is the "sacrament" of the mystery of Jesus.

A second spiritual meaning of scripture is the *tropological* (from the Greek *tropos,* meaning "way of life", "life-style", "manner of believing and behaving"). The tropological sense of scripture points to the individual Christian, to his way of life. The letter of James uses the tropological meaning of Abraham's obedience in offering Isaac on the altar to tell us that in our own lives "faith without good deeds is useless" (2:20-23).

Just as the allegorical meaning refers to Christ and the Church, so the tropological meaning refers to the Christian in relation to Jesus in daily life in the Church; it also refers to the christian community, to the Church in its daily life. The mysteries of faith expressed in the allegorical meaning are lived out daily by the Christian — and this is the tropological meaning. For example, everyone must live the mystery of the birth of Jesus by being born again of the Spirit; and just as Jesus grew in age and grace and wisdom, we are called to grow in the same way. The tropological sense, then, flows from the doctrinal or allegorical sense; it refers to the living out of the doctrine, to the becoming-real in everyday living of the mystery that is prefigured allegorically.

With the rise of medieval monastic theology, tropology has a particularly important role in understanding scripture and in applying it to daily life. Paradise becomes a figure of the cloister; Peter's words about a royal priesthood and a holy nation (I Pet 2:9) are applied to the monastic life; Babylon and Jerusalem stand for the world and the monastery. Bernard of Clairvaux sees in the six jars at the Cana wedding reception the water for the six purifications of the monk: silence, singing the Psalms, manual labor, chastity, fasting, and night vigils.

Henri de Lubac points out the particular importance of the Song of Songs in the christian tradition of the spiritual interpretation of scripture. Commentaries on the Song of Songs stress its tropological meaning, its meaning for the life of the Church and for the life of each Christian. He writes:

> This small book is in fact understood from one end to the other as expressing the heart of the revelation everywhere diffused in scripture: it celebrates symbolically the great mystery of love, the union of God and man prefigured in Israel and

fulfilled through the Incarnation of the
Word.[6]

Although opinions are greatly divided, many contemporary commentators see in the Song of Songs a
collection of secular love songs, and understand the
literal meaning as an exaltation of the love between
man and woman.[7] In any case, from the beginning,
in the whole judeo-christian tradition, the Song of
Songs has been interpreted as expressing the union
between God and his Church and between God and
the believer. The christian tradition remains in
continuity with the earlier Jewish interpretations,
but now, especially with Origen, Gregory the Great,
and Bernard of Clairvaux, the Song of Songs is read
as the story of the union between Jesus and his
Church and between Jesus and each Christian. There
are not two lines of interpretation − one applying
the Song to the Church and the other to the
Christian − but one clear line that emphasizes sometimes one and sometimes the other, and in which
both stand in intimate relationship. This relationship
is that between the allegorical sense and the
tropological sense, between the Song as showing the
union of love between Jesus and his people and as
showing the union, especially in prayer, between
Jesus and each person. Even in the many interpretations in the Middle Ages that apply the Song of
Songs to Mary, the reading is the same: Mary is seen
as in the Church or at its summit, and as an example
of union with Jesus.[8]

According to Origen, the author of the Song of
Songs under the image of the lovers inspires the soul
with the love of heaven and of the things of God
and teaches it to progress in divine union along the

path of love.[9] This interpretation flowered in later
writers and especially in the homilies of St Bernard
on the Song of Songs and in the teachings on prayer
of John of the Cross, who wanted as he died to
listen to it one last time.[10] In the Prologue to his
Spiritual Canticle, John of the Cross writes that in
the Song of Songs,

> . . . the Holy Spirit, unable to express the
> fullness of his meaning in ordinary words,
> utters mysteries in strange figures and
> likenesses. The saintly doctors, no matter
> how much they have said or will say, can
> never furnish an exhaustive explanation of
> these figures and comparisons, since the
> abundant meanings of the Holy Spirit
> cannot be caught in words.[11]

In the liturgy for the feast of St Mary Magdalene,
the Church encourages us to see the Song of Songs'
passage where the girl rises and goes through the city
searching for her lover ("I will seek him whom my
heart loves") and finds him ("I found him whom my
heart loves; I held him fast") as allegorically pre-
figuring Mary Magdalene's search for and encounter
with Jesus after the resurrection (Song of Songs
3:1-4; Jn 20:11-18). And it leads us to read both
tropologically, understanding both the Song of
Songs and John's account of the post-resurrection
encounter as images of the Christian's searching for
and finding Jesus in prayer.[12]

The fourth meaning of scripture, beyond the
literal, the allegorical (or doctrinal), and the
tropological (or christian-life) meanings, is the
anagogical (from the Greek *anagogé*, "a rising up",

"a coming to life again") meaning of scripture. The anagogical (or "resurrection") meaning of the Bible points to the ultimate future, to the life of the world to come. It leads us to the contemplation of the realities of heaven, and shows us life in this world in the light of the world to come. The Letter to the Hebrews uses the anagogical meaning to scripture when it understands the Church as the heavenly Jerusalem and Christians as citizens of the new Jerusalem in heaven (Heb 12:22). In this way, the anagogical sense completes the allegorical; allegorically, the Church on earth is the new Jerusalem, and anagogically she already belongs to the heavenly Jerusalem.

For clarity, we can apply the four meanings of scripture to the Jerusalem temple. The temple of Jerusalem signifies:

(1) the historical temple (literal sense);
(2) the risen Jesus ("destroy this temple and in three days I will raise it up"), and also the Church (allegorical or doctrinal sense);
(3) the individual Christian, or his heart, as a temple of the Holy Spirit (tropological or christian-life sense);
(4) the New Jerusalem that will come down from heaven (anagogical or "resurrection" sense).

Jesus gives the pattern of the four meanings of scripture in his interpretation of the manna in the desert (Jn 6:25-66). The manna that God gave his people in the Exodus (literal meaning) prefigured the true bread of life, Jesus (doctrinal meaning), who calls me now to eat his body and drink his blood (christian-life meaning) so that he will raise me up on the last day ("resurrection" meaning). He uses the same pattern of the four senses of the Bible when talking to Nicodemus: "As Moses lifted up the serpent in the desert" (literal sense), so "the Son of Man must be lifted up" (doctrinal) "so that every-one who believes" (christian-life) "may have eternal life in him" ("resurrection") (Jn 3:13-15).

Paul uses the spiritual meaning of scripture when he understands the slave Hagar and the free woman Sarah as types of the Old Covenant and the New Covenant: "This can be regarded as an allegory, the women stand for the two covenants" (Gal 4:24). The allegorical or doctrinal sense gives rise to the tropological or Christian-life sense. Because we are children of the free woman, the "Jerusalem above" (doctrinal), Paul encourages us to live accordingly: "When Christ freed us, he meant us to remain free; stand firm therefore and do not submit again to the yoke of slavery" (5:1). For we are "children of the promise" (4:29), and we look to those rewards that righteousness hopes for (5:5); this is the anagogical or "resurrection" sense.

The spiritual sense of scripture sees the reality of Jesus and his Church as:

(1) foretold in the Old Testament;

(2) fulfilled in the New Testament, in what we hold in *faith;*

(3) lived out in Christian life, in *love;*

(4) and finalized in the glory in which we *hope.*

The Spiritual Meaning of Scripture Today

Some would hold that the spiritual interpretation of scripture, although widespread in the early Church and down through the medieval period as well as in both Protestantism and Catholicism in the seventeenth century is too old-fashioned for today, not sufficiently scientific.[13] However, the use of the spiritual meaning of scripture in personal prayer, in preaching and writing, and in the liturgy, and the belief that the Spirit speaks to each Christian in his own life situation through the Bible, are firmly established in the practice of the Church.

Henri de Lubac has focussed christian attention once again on the age-old belief in the two-fold inspiration by the Holy Spirit with regard to the Bible: that scripture is God's inspired word, and that the Spirit inspires those who read it in faith. The Bible is story-of-life-in-the-Spirit: the story of the people of Israel, marked by God's prophetic word and by continuous wisdom; the story of Jesus; the story of the early Church. Lived and recorded in the Spirit, the story needs to be read in the Spirit. The same Holy Spirit who inspired scripture leads us today to read and to understand it. The Holy Spirit "is the inner source of spiritual understanding."[14] De Lubac tells us that we should not imagine

> . . . that the sacred text holds a series of already formed meanings waiting to be more or less discovered. The Spirit imparts to the text a limitless power, and so the text has indefinite possibilities of depths. No less than the world, scripture, that "other world", has not been created once and for all; the Spirit still "creates",

94

each day so to speak, in the measure that
he "unfolds" [scripture's meaning] . . .
and broadens the understanding of him
who receives it.[15]

The Spirit shows us the unity of the literal and
spiritual meanings, and he shows us Jesus in the
whole Bible.[16]

Jesus Christ gives the unity to scripture
because he is its purpose and its fullness.
Everything in it is related to him. He is,
finally, its only Subject. He is, we might
say, its whole interpretation . . . And he is
also its Interpreter. It is he and he alone
who explains it to us, and in explaining it,
he explains himself.[17]

Scripture's spiritual meaning, then, is made clear by
the Lord through his Spirit. It is arrived at in
personal relationship with him and in the Holy
Spirit -- in other words, in prayer. David Stanley
suggests that scripture can be used in personal
prayer and in prayerful reading by following two
simple steps. The first is to read the passage according to its literal meaning. Secondly, I "must reflect
with faith upon the literal sense already uncovered,
in order to hear what the risen Christ is saying
through his Spirit as one reads a particular passage at
a given moment."[18] This listening to the Lord is
"The obedience of faith" (Rom 1:5; see 15:7), and
puts me in relationship with him so that he can
explain the scripture to me as it applies to me here
and now.

A common public example of the prayerful use of

the spiritual sense of the Bible can be seen in charismatic prayer meetings. In the context of the group prayer, a scripture text read aloud finds immediately a spiritual meaning, perhaps made clear by a comment or a prayer, or perhaps immediately understood by all from the context in which it is read. Sometimes, after a text is read, interpretations expressed in teaching, prophecy, or prayer follow at all three levels – allegorical, tropological, anagogical – drawing from the text truth to be-believed, truth-to-be-done, and truth-to-be-hoped-for. Far from being "fundamentalist" in the pejorative sense, the use of the Bible in most such prayer meetings is highly informed by the long christian tradition of the spiritual interpretation of scripture.

To pray with scripture by reading it for its spiritual meaning does not of course require any knowledge of terms such as "allegorical" or "tropological". To look for the spiritual sense of scripture means to let the Lord speak to me through a scripture passage. It means to take a text for the day; or even, sometimes, after praying for guidance, to open the Bible at random to look for the word God has for me now. And it means seeing what the Lord might be saying to me in that passage, praying about it, taking it seriously and personally.

The Lord calls me to abide in him, and he wants his words to abide in me (Jn 15:7).[19] I can listen prayerfully to the Lord's voice as he speaks to me through scripture, interpreting it for me personally, guiding my understanding through his Holy Spirit. I can say in the words of the Song of Songs, "I hear the voice of my beloved" (2:8). And when the Lord speaks, comments William of Saint-Thierry on this text, "what he speaks is himself to the Bride, and so in himself he makes known to her all that he wants her to know."[20] "He begins in her something of himself, so that she can be in him."[21] And in response I can pray to be more in the Lord, to abide more in him in love:

> Set me like a seal on your heart,
>   like a seal on your arm.
> For love is strong as death,
>   jealousy relentless as Hell.
> The flash of it is a flash of fire,
>   a flame of the Lord himself.
>
> (Song of Songs 8:6)

Notes

[1] *Catholicism. Christ and the Common Destiny of Man*, trans. L. Sheppard (London: Burns and Oates, 1962), was first published as *Catholicisme, Les aspects sociaux du dogme* (Paris: Cerf, 1938).

[2] De Lubac's scholarly studies in the patristic and medieval development of exegesis are for the most part not translated into English: *Histoire et Esprit. L'intelligence de l'Ecriture d'après Origène* (Paris: Aubier, 1950); *Exégèse médiévale, Les quattre sens de l'Ecriture,* 4 vols. (Paris: Aubier, 1959, 1961, 1964, and 1969). The conclusion of *Histoire et Esprit* and some parts of *Exégèse médiévale* have been brought together and published in one volume: *L'Ecriture dans la tradition* (Paris: Aubier, 1966); translated by L. O'Neill as *The Sources of Revelation* (New York: Herder and Herder, 1968).

[3] Quoted in David M. Stanley, "A Suggested Approach to *Lectio Divina*", *American Benedictine Review,* 23 (1972), p. 441.

[4] *Histoire et Esprit, op. cit.,* p. 179.

[5] *Exégèse médiévale, op. cit.,* vol. Ia, p. 305; see *Catholicism, op. cit.,* pp. 85-90.

[6] *Exégèse médiévale, op. cit.,* vol. Ia, p. 560; what follows is taken from pp. 560-562; see also *Histoire et Esprit, op. cit.,* pp. 191-194.

[7] See the commentary by Roland E. Murphy, O.Carm., in *The Jerome Biblical Commentary* (London: Chapman, 1968), vol. II, pp. 506-510, and his articles in the *Catholic Biblical Quarterly*, 16 (1954), 1-11, and 39 (1977), 482-496.

[8] See H. de Lubac, *Méditation sur l'Eglise* (Paris: Aubier, 1953), pp. 306-324; *The Eternal Feminine*, trans. R. Hague (London: Collins, 1971), pp. 107-230.

[9] Prologue to his commentary on the Song of Songs, quoted in *Histoire et Esprit, op. cit.*, p. 192.

[10] *Exégèse médiévale, op. cit.*, vol. II, p. 500.

[11] *The Collected Works of St. John of the Cross*, trans. K. Kavanaugh and O. Rodriquez (Washington D.C.: Institute of Carmelite Studies, 1973), pp. 408-409.

[12] See A. Feuillet, *Le mystère de l'amour divin dans la théologie Johannique* (Paris: Garbalda, 1972), p. 231.

[13] See for example Raymond E. Brown, S.S., "Hermeneutics", in *The Jerome Biblical Commentary, op. cit.*, vol. II, pp. 610-615; Father Brown feels that any more-than-literal exegesis has "real dangers against which one must take precautions" (p. 615). The chief danger, it seems to me, lies in three temptations: (1) to over-emphasize the literal meaning and to belittle the spiritual; (2) to stress the importance of the spiritual sense in such a way that the need for study and modern technical exegesis in arriving at a better understanding of the literal sense is depreciated; (3) to separate the literal and spiritual meanings by taking the search for the literal meaning out of the realm of faith.

[14] *Exégèse médiévale, op. cit.*, vol. I, p. 355.

[15] *Ibid.*, p. 654.

[16] John Duns Scotus: "The very spirit of the letter is Christ", *In Johannem*, Migne, Latin Series, vol. 122, col. 331; quoted by de Lubac in *Exégèse médiévale, op. cit.*, vol. I, p. 321.

[17] *Exégèse médiévale, op. cit.*, vol. I, pp. 322-323.

[18] Stanley, *op. cit.*, pp. 454-455. For a book that stresses the use of scripture in prayer, see: Andre Louf, *Teach Us to Pray* (New York: Paulist, 1977).

[19] See John 5:38; I John 2:14 and 24.

[20] *Supra Cantica Cantorum*, Migne, Latin Series, vol. 180, col. 52.

[21] *Ibid.*

III. BASIC WAYS OF PRAYING

What should I do when I pray? How should I pray? What should I pray about?

In prayer, rigid programming is counterproductive, because the Lord resists manipulation. "Back-seat driving" will get me nowhere; I am not behind the wheel. When I pray, the Spirit prays in me; my prayer is first of all God's gift, his action in me. I need, then, docility to this action. Prayer is like dancing; the Lord leads, and I follow. So I need a certain stillness and a kind of inner flexibility so that he can guide my prayer the way he wants to. I need to abide in him, to remain in him. I should pray in whatever way I feel comfortable-with-the-Lord, in whatever way I find facility or ease in relating to him, in remaining in him. The Lord will lead me in different ways at different times. For example, he may lead me to ask him for what I need, or to praise him, or to thank him, or just to be centered on him in silence.

Chapter Eight
ASKING

"I am the vine and you are the branches", the Lord tells us. "If you abide in me, and my words abide in you, ask whatever you will and it shall be done for you" (Jn 15:7). "Ask, and you will receive, that your joy may be full" (Jn 16:24); "If you ask anything in my name, I will do it" (Jn 14:14). These promises seem exaggerated, but the Lord's teaching in the other three Gospels is equally strong and explicit.[1]

> Ask, and it will be given you. Seek and you will find; knock and it will be opened to you. For everyone who asks receives, and he who seeks finds, and to him who knocks it will be opened. What man of you, if his son asks him for bread, will give him a stone? Or if he asks for a fish will give him a serpent? If you then, who are evil, know how to give good gifts to your children, how much more will your Father who is in heaven give good things to those who ask him!
>
> (Mt 7:7-11; Lk 11:9-13)

The point of the two parables about asking a friend at midnight for three loaves of bread (Lk 11:5-8), and about the widow and the judge (Lk 18:1-8) is the efficacy of sincere and persistent prayer of petition.

A further point of Jesus' teaching on asking in prayer is the importance of praying with faith, with trust in the goodness and the power of God. "Whatever you ask in prayer, believe that you receive it, and you will" (Mk 11:24); "Whatever you ask in prayer, you will receive, if you have faith" (Mt 21:22).[2] Jesus' healings are often in response to the faith of the person asking. This prayer-in-faith goes out to the Lord in trust, not only believing in the power of his love, but believing that the Lord wants to, can, and will help in this particular situation now. The Letter of James, echoing Jesus' teaching, encourages us to ask in faith, with no doubting, for "he who doubts is like a wave of the sea that is driven and tossed by the wind"; we should not suppose that "a double-minded man, unstable in all his ways, will receive anything from the Lord" (Jas 1:6-7).

What should we pray for? We can pray for our own needs and for the needs of others. We can "cast our cares on the Lord", putting each worry and preoccupation in his hands. We can pray for our friends and our families. We can change our distractions into prayer by lifting up the content of those distractions to the Lord in prayer of petition.

We can ask for material things; but spiritual gifts are more important, and we should "earnestly desire" them (I Cor 14:1). Most of all, we should desire and ask for union with God, that he bless us by taking us more to himself. As prayer grows and matures, the "asking" aspect becomes simply an all-enveloping desire for the Lord, a hunger for God that for some at times can take an acute form. Several christian writers have seen the symbol of this in Jacob wrestling with the angel (Gen 32:24-28; Hos 12:3-4).

Jacob is alone in the dark facing a God whom he does not fully recognize. He wrestles with the mysterious figure and will not lèt him go until the "angel" has blessed him. As dawn breaks, God blesses Jacob and gives him a new name, a new destiny and a new way of relating to God. Only afterwards, in awe at having been face to face with God, does Jacob realize the importance of what has happened. That his life has changed is evident right away in his unpredictably joyful reconciliation with Esau, the brother with whom he fought in their mother's womb and whose heritage he took.

Patristic and medieval authors often understand the encounter with Jacob and the angel tropologically, as a symbol of the Christian's encounter with the Lord in prayer.[3] The Lord lets himself be conquered because he wants to give me his blessing,[4] so that I may have a greater fullness of reconciliation with him and with my brothers and sisters.

Eventually my asking-in-prayer should mature into a quiet and peaceful yearning for the Lord, an abiding in him that looks for nothing but a still closer and more intimate union. Yet, there will always be times when I will turn to him to ask him for help for myself or for others.

Petitionary prayer for others, particularly asking for God's grace for them, fills the letters of Paul.[5] That I can do this and should is part of the christian doctrine of the "communion of saints" – that we make up one Body of Christ, one living temple of God, one vine. I can pray for others whether they know I do or not, and in their presence or absence. And if we pray together, then our prayer has a special efficacy (Mt 18:19-20). And, in any case, as St Augustine has put it, "God has willed that in life's battle we do more by our prayer than by our own efforts."[6]

Notes

[1] An excellent scholarly study in Spanish on "prayer of petition" in the Gospels is: José Caba, *La Oración de petición* (Rome: Biblical Institute Press, 1974).

[2] See Mt 17:20-21; Mk 9:23-24 and 28-29.

[3] For example, Rabanus Maurus (ninth century): "This can be usefully understood tropologically . . . The angel, in this case, stands for the Lord; and Jacob, who wrestles with the angel, stands for the soul of any just man giving himself to contemplation . . ." *Commentariorum in Genesim,* book 3, chapter 21, in Migne, Latin Series, vol. 107, col. 610-611; see vol. III, col. 42.

[4] Augustine, Sermon 122, in Migne, Latin Series, vol. 38, col. 681.

[5] See for example: II Thess 1:11-12 and 2:16 — 3:1; I Thess 3:13 and 5:23-25; II Cor 13:13; Phil 1:8-11; see also I Tim 2:1-7.

[6] *Contra Julianum opus imperfectum,* book 6, chapter 15, in Migne, Latin Series, vol. 45, col. 1535.

Chapter Nine

THANKING AND PRAISING

Ignatius Loyola calls the last of his "spiritual exercises" the "Contemplation for Obtaining Love"; he intends it to be a prayer to help us to grow in the gift of love for Jesus Christ.[1] More than a meditation or a way of praying, Ignatius understands the "Contemplation for Obtaining Love" as a whole way of seeing reality, as a prayerful approach to all of life. He presents it as a perspective for all who want to be "contemplatives in action", finding the Lord in all things.[2] Ignatius observes, first of all, that love is manifested in deeds rather than in words, and that those who love one another exchange gifts. Then he asks us to consider four successive points: (1) the gifts the Lord gives us: all of creation, our redemption, his Spirit, family, friends, health, and so on; (2) that the Lord is present in his gifts, for the giver gives himself in his gift; (3) that he is further present in every gift through his creative influence that holds it in existence; (4) that all blessings come from the Lord. Considering the Lord's gifts, his presence in them and his self-giving, I can thank him, explicitly and for specific gifts. Through this prayer of thanks, I grow in love of the Lord.

Some of the Psalms are prayers of thanksgiving,[3] and the historical books of the Old Testament have canticles of thanksgiving. St Paul in his letters frequently thanks God, especially for spiritual gifts and for his friends. Giving thanks to the Lord for his gifts is a traditional and common prayer because it effectively takes me to the Lord in referring his gifts back to him gratitude.

When I praise God, on the other hand, I applaud him because he is God. "Praise is the point at which thanksgiving becomes thanking God for being God."[4] I can praise the Lord for his goodness, his love, his wisdom, his infinite greatness. I can praise him for his creation or for any part of it, for his saving acts, and for anything because he is the Lord of everything. I am applauding him for being the kind of Lord who is like he is, who has created all these things, who acts as he acts. Praise acclaims God, claps its hands, says "Alleluia!" which means, "Praise the Lord!"

Many of the Psalms are prayers of praise,[5] and both the Old and New Testaments have several hymns of praise.[6] The letters of Paul contain frequent bursts of praise, and Paul tells us that we who have "hoped in Christ have been destined and appointed to live for the praise of his glory" (Eph 1:12). Christians glorify God in the Acts of the Apostles,[7] and God and the Lamb are praised in heaven in the visions of John's Apocalypse.[8]

Litanies are praise, glorifying God by giving him names that praise him. Marius Victorinus' third hymn to the Trinity is a litany of praise.

> God, Lord, Holy Spirit, O blessed Trinity.
> Father, Son, Paraclete, O blessed Trinity ...
> Source, River, Watering, O blessed Trinity.
> In three, triple, but one, O blessed Trinity.
> Existence, Life, Knowledge, O blessed Trinity.

> Love, Grace, Communication, O blessed
> Trinity.
> God is love, Christ is grace, the Holy Spirit
> is communication, O blessed Trinity ...
> True light, true light of true light, true
> illumination, O blessed Trinity ...
> Seed, tree, fruit, O blessed Trinity.
> All things from One, all things through
> One, all things in One, O blessed
> Trinity ...[9]

The litany of the Sacred Heart combines praise with
petition for mercy:

> ... Heart of Jesus, sacred temple of God,
> have mercy on us ...
> Heart of Jesus, house of God and gate of
> heaven, have mercy on us ...
> Heart of Jesus, full of goodness and love,
> have mercy on us ...
> Heart of Jesus, King and center of all
> hearts, have mercy on us ...
> Heart of Jesus, our life and resurrection,
> have mercy on us ...
> Heart of Jesus, our peace and reconcilia-
> tion, have mercy on us ...

Praise, like all prayer, is a gift. One form that the
gift of praise takes, frequently in the pentecostal
churches and charismatic movements but often too
outside them, is the gift of tongues. Praising God in
tongues is a kind of babbling to the Lord, a sort of
pre-speech like that of an infant who cannot yet
speak but who makes non-sensical sounds. Praising
God in tongues is non-conceptual vocal prayer,

109

analogous to being silently and without concepts before the Lord in an attitude of praise. It is analogous also to the repetitive part of a litany of praise ("O blessed Trinity", "Heart of Jesus"); repetition frees the mind from concern with meaning so that it can focus more on the One being praised.

The gift in the gift of tongues is not, of course, to make incomprehensible sounds, but that the sounds be praise. Peter Hocken has expressed it this way:

> Much misunderstanding and confusion stem from the focus on the language aspect (any prayer of praise may not be linguistically impressive!) and from treating this phenomenon as extraordinary. . . . From the nature of the case, anyone whose prayer has become predominantly the prayer of praise is near to praying in tongues; and it is really as simple as asking God for the extra push and letting it come . . . Of its nature, it requires a letting go of our self-control, of our tight grip on ourselves. It is within prayer a form of dying to self and rising to new life.[10]

The principal use of praying in tongues is in private personal prayer, and many find it a good way to begin their daily personal "quiet time with the Lord". Group praying and singing in tongues can be seen at almost any charismatic prayer meeting. But the gift is hardly restricted to the charismatic movement, and many people who do not go to prayer meetings use the gift in their own daily prayer.

110

Prayer of praise, like prayer of petition, tends to broaden out into a relationship with the Lord that includes everything because it is one of continuous praise for all things. The Lord can teach me to praise him for difficulties, because in his providence for me he writes straight with crooked lines; and to praise him even when I might feel negatively, because although I have moods he remains always infinitely worthy of praise.

> Looking only at the good side of every situation is often a dangerous way of trying to escape the reality of it. When we praise God we thank him *for* our situation, not in spite of it. We are not trying to avoid our dilemmas, rather Jesus Christ is showing us a way to overcome them. There is a ladder of praise and I believe that everyone without exception can begin to praise God right now in whatever situation he may find himself.[11]

Notes

[1] *Spiritual Exercises, op. cit.*, numbers 230-237. In this "contemplation" Ignatius speaks of "God", but nearly always he means Jesus Christ.

[2] See J. Danielou, "Ignatian Vision of the Universe and Man", *Cross Currents*, 4 (1954), 357-366; R. Roth, "Contemplation in Action", *Review for Religious*, 21 (1962), 531-540; E. Coreth, "In actione contemplativus", *Theology Digest*, 3 (1955), 37-45; J.F. Conwell, *Contemplation in Action* (Spokane: Gonzaga, 1957).

[3] See, for example, Psalms 105, 106, 107, 111, 136, 138.

[4] Peter Hocken, *You He Made Alive* (London: Darton, Longman, and Todd, 1974), p. 79. Good books on the place of praise in christian life are those of Merlin R. Carothers,

for example, *From Prison to Praise* (Plainfield, N.J.: Logos, 1970).

[5] See, for example, Psalms 8, 100, 103, 104, 113, 117, 135, 136, 145, 146, and 148.

[6] See, for example, Is chapter 25; Is 42:10-13; Nah 1:2-8; and, in the Gospels, especially that of Lk: 1:46-55; 1:68-79; 2:13-14; 2:28-32.

[7] 3:8-9; 4:21; 10:46; 11:18; 19:17; 21:20.

[8] 4:8-11; 11:16-17; 19:4.

[9] *Marii Victorini opera, Corpus scriptorum ecclesiasticorum latinorum,* vol. 83, pp. 294-305; Marius Victorinus, *Sources chrétiennes,* no. 68, pp. 634-653.

[10] *You He Made Alive, op. cit.,* pp. 83 and 82. On praying in tongues, see Larry Christensen, *Speaking in Tongues* (Minneapolis: Dimension, 1968); the classical theological study on the gift of tongues is Francis A. Sullivan, "Speaking in Tongues", *Lumen Vitae,* 31 (1976), 145-170.

[11] Merlin R. Carothers, *From Prison to Praise, op. cit.,* p. 106.

Chapter Ten
SILENTLY ABIDING

The Lord can lead us into a prayer that is so simple that little or nothing seems to happen, like the prayer of the peasant who, when Jean Vianney asked him what he did when he sat alone in the church, replied, "I just look at Him, and He looks at me." This prayer of simple regard is a gift of abiding in the Lord in prayer. It is prayer with few or no words, just a loving, or a yearning, or an attitude of praise or thanksgiving, or simply a silent being-present-to-the-Lord, a remaining in him, quiet abiding.

This simple prayer in which I basically do little except abide in the Lord can be the most important activity of my day. And I should not let the busy-ness of the contemporary world and its preoccupation for "results" dictate otherwise. Perhaps because of the feverish work-orientation in western culture, there has always existed in our theology a current that devalues simultaneously God's transcendence and his immanence in the world, reducing the reality we live to the secular city, that minimizes the proclamation of God's judgment and of his Spirit breaking into our lives as Chicken-little crying that the sky is falling, and that reduces the search for the true self in prayer to narcissistic navel-gazing. Do not listen to the voices that call us to be busy about many things, because only one thing is necessary: to sit at Jesus' feet looking at him and listening to him

(Lk 11:39-42).

To rest silently in the Lord is a traditional christian way of praying. In recent years some teachers and writers have borrowed from other traditions, especially from Buddhism and Hinduism, in order to adapt their methods so as to aid christian prayer — especially to aid the prayer of simple regard, the prayer of simply abiding in the Lord. A method that contains what is best in the prayer methods of the eastern spiritualities is that of "centering prayer".[1] In some respects like zen and yoga techniques, it nevertheless is completely christian, based on the fourteenth-century spiritual classic *The Cloud of Unknowing*[2] and inspired by Thomas Merton's idea that the way to come into living contact with God is to go to one's center and from there pass into God.

The method of the centering prayer is concisely described by Trappist Abbot Thomas Keating:

> Take up a position that will enable you to sit still. Close your eyes . . . Then slow down the normal flow of thoughts by thinking just one thought. Choose a sacred word of one or two syllables with which you feel comfortable. It will be the sign of your intention to open yourself interiorly to the mystery of God's enveloping presence. Keep thinking this sacred word. When you become aware that you are off on some other thought, return gently to this word.[3]

Father Basil Pennington recommends that "at the beginning of the prayer we take a minute or two to quiet down, and then move in faith to God dwelling in our depths"; and that we then take up a single simple word, such as the name of Jesus, and "begin to let it repeat itself within".[4] He also strongly recommends two periods of this contemplative prayer during the course of the day; twenty minutes might be a good length of time to begin with, and some will feel drawn to lengthen this to periods of twenty-five or thirty or thirty-five minutes.

May the Lord give us his peace, and in his peace teach our hearts "to commune silently in a living union with him", in a "complete silent oblation of self and an entire surrender to God".[5] And may he bless us and keep us and lead us in the ways of his Spirit.

Notes

[1] On "centering prayer", see M. Basil Pennington, *Daily We Touch Him* (New York: Doubleday, 1977); "Centering Prayer – Prayer of Quiet", *Review for Religious*, 35 (1976), 651-662. See also, Thomas Keating, "Cultivating the Centering Prayer", *Review for Religious*, 36 (1977), 10-15.

[2] There are several editions of this work, four of them in paperback.

[3] "Cultivating the Centering Prayer", *op. cit.*, p. 11.

[4] "Centering Prayer – Prayer of Quiet", *op. cit.*, pp. 657 and 660.

[5] Karl Rahner, *Encounters with Silence* (Westminster: Newman, 1965), p. 15.

Afterword
THE VINE AND THE BRANCHES

Throughout writing this book, Jn 15:1-9 has been in my mind, in the background, like an old song that hums itself behind more occupying thoughts, or like a shadowy figure moving from tree to tree in the back of the woods along the river bank. "I am the vine, and you are the branches." (15:5) "Abide in me, as I abide in you" (15:4). So, in the foreword, and appearing here and there in the subsequent chapters, has been a tropological or "christian-life" interpretation of the vine and branches passage. Specifically, my reading of the text has been in terms of the conscious union of the Christian with Jesus Christ in prayer.

But a "christian-life" reading of scripture comes from a doctrinal (or allegorical) interpretation, which in turn is based on the literal reading. I would like to comment briefly on these two meanings of Jn 15:1-9, the literal and the allegorical.

The Structure and Literal Meaning
The literary structure of the text is not linear (A B C D E) but a chiasm, a kind of sandwich (A B C B A). In this case, however, the first and center verses are parallel. The text can be arranged to show the parallelisms:

I am the real vine (1a),
    and my father is the gardener. He cuts off

117

> any of my branches that does not bear
> fruit, but any that bears fruit he trims
> clean to make it bear more fruit. You are
> clean already, thanks to the word I have
> spoken to you (1b-3).
>> Remain in me as I remain in you (4a).
>>> Just as a branch cannot bear fruit by itself
>>> without remaining on the vine, so neither
>>> can you bear fruit without remaining in
>>> me (4b).

I am the vine; you are the branches.
He who remains in me and I in him is
the one who bears much fruit, for apart
from me you can do nothing (5).

>>> If a man does not remain in me, he is like
>>> a branch, cast off and withered, which
>>> they collect and throw into the fire to be
>>> burned (6).
>> If you remain in me and my words remain in
>> you, ask for whatever you want and it will
>> be done for you (7).
>> My Father has been glorified in this: in your
>> bearing much fruit and becoming my
>> disciples (8).

Verse 9 marks a transition and combines a main idea
of the following section, "As the Father has loved
me so I have loved you", with the principal directive
of the preceding section, "Remain in my love". The
central and key idea, verse 5, stands in the center of
the text, surrounded by parallels that develop it.

The literal meaning is a metaphor. The first or
face meaning of the words is that Jesus is metaphorically the true vine, just as he is the "true light"
(Jn 1:9) in contrast with the creation-story light

(Gen 1:3), the "true bread from heaven" (Jn 6:32) as compared with the manna of the desert march (Ps 77:24-25), the "true son of God" (I Jn 5:20) in comparison with Israel as the son of God (Hos 11:1; Ex 4:23).[2] Jesus stands in contrast with these Old Testament figures, and he fulfills them; John's Gospel reads them according to their allegorical (christian doctrine) meaning. In the same way, Jesus stands in contrast to and fulfills Israel as God's vine, "a luxuriant vine" (Hos 10:1; see Is 5:1-7) "of fully genuine stock" that "degenerated into a wild vine" (Jer 2:21; see 6:9) to be "put in the fire" (Ezek 15:6; see 17:5-10; 19:10-12).

Notice that the literal meaning of Jn 15:1-9 involves an allegorical reading of the corresponding Old Testament passages because it fulfills them. But its *own* allegorical (or doctrinal) meaning issues from the literal meaning. The allegorical sense of the vine and branches passage is what it teaches us about the Church, about christian community.

The Allegorical Meaning

Jesus, the genuine vine, does not abolish Israel as God's vine. On the contrary, Israel as vine is an allegory of Jesus as true vine, and he fulfills it as the perfection of the vine that is Israel. And, by the very nature of the image, the vine includes Jesus' disciples; the vine stands for the new Israel, the Church. We belong to the vine; we form part of it, its branches. But Jesus is not just the stalk; he is the whole vine of which we too are part. The vine metaphor communicates the same reality as does Paul's image of the Church as the Body of Christ. The vine, like the Body of Christ in Paul's letters, is the universal Church and, also, every local church, and by extension every christian community. This is the doctrinal or allegorical meaning of the passage.

In early christian art, the vine often grows out of the cross of Christ. Sometimes the crucifix is represented as a simple cross, sometimes as a chalice with the vine growing from inside the cup, and sometimes Christ crucified is symbolized by the great cluster of grapes hung from a pole carried by the two scouts returning from their exploration of the promised land (Num 13:23). All these allegorical symbols find their literary equivalents in the writings of the Fathers of the Church.

Often, too, the vine resembles a tree of life that spreads out so that the birds of the air can shelter in its shade (Mk 4:30-32). The twelfth-century Roman church of St Clement, built over the third century St Clement's and with obvious efforts to return to primitive christian architecture, has over the main altar a huge mosaic of a wide-spreading vine growing out of the cross of Jesus crucified.[3] The vine is an acanthus plant, used in classical art as a tree of life. Deer drink from water flowing in four streams from the vine's center.[4] Numerous birds, including two in cages (representing the soul and the body), peacocks (symbol of the resurrection), and even a duck, walk under, perch on, and fly through the vine. The vine's branches frame doctors of the Church, saints, ordinary persons, flowers, fruits, rustic scenes that stand for the Church (a shepherd with sheep, a woman feeding chickens), and other things. The cross reaches up to the heavens, from which comes the Father's hand outstretched to crown Jesus on the cross. Along the base of the mosaic runs the inscription, "To this vine we compare the Church of Christ which the law dries up and the cross renders

120

flourishing."

Because we are branches on the vine, in Jesus, our prayer always has a community dimension. Abiding in Jesus, we abide together, united in him. His same Spirit lives in our hearts and makes us one. Thomas Merton, in his hermitage, found his brothers and sisters in Jesus. Pierre Teilhard de Chardin's union in prayer with the risen Jesus led him to find Christ in the world and in everyone he met. And Henri de Lubac has reminded us of the constancy of christian teaching in its emphasis on the community dimension of abiding in the Lord.

Notes

[1] I am following the translation of Raymond Brown, *The Gospel according to John. The Anchor Bible* (New York: Doubleday, 1970), 649-650; an excellent commentary on Jn 15:1-17 follows (pp. 659-684). Note that verses 12-17 form a chiasm with no center; 14 and 15 are parallel, as are 13 and 16 and 12 and 17.

[2] See David Stanley, "I Am the Genuine Vine", *The Bible Today*, (1963), 464-491.

[3] The concept is copied from early mosaics, probably specifically from one in the Lateran basilica.

[4] See Jn 4:10-14; Ps 42:1-2; Ezek 47:1-2; Is 49:10; Zech 14:8; Rev 7:17; 21:6; 22:17.